Cambridge Elements

Elements in Music Since 1945
edited by
Mervyn Cooke
University of Nottingham

MARIACHI IN THE TWENTY-FIRST CENTURY

Donald A. Westbrook
San José State University

Shaftesbury Road, Cambridge CB2 8EA, United Kingdom

One Liberty Plaza, 20th Floor, New York, NY 10006, USA

477 Williamstown Road, Port Melbourne, VIC 3207, Australia

314–321, 3rd Floor, Plot 3, Splendor Forum, Jasola District Centre,
New Delhi – 110025, India

103 Penang Road, #05–06/07, Visioncrest Commercial, Singapore 238467

Cambridge University Press is part of Cambridge University Press & Assessment,
a department of the University of Cambridge.

We share the University's mission to contribute to society through the pursuit of education, learning and research at the highest international levels of excellence.

www.cambridge.org
Information on this title: www.cambridge.org/9781009461337

DOI: 10.1017/9781009461320

When citing this work, please include a reference to the DOI 10.1017/9781009461320

First published 2024

A catalogue record for this publication is available from the British Library.

ISBN 978-1-009-46133-7 Hardback
ISBN 978-1-009-46136-8 Paperback
ISSN 2632-7791 (online)
ISSN 2632-7783 (print)

Additional resources for this publication at www.cambridge.org/Westbrook

Mariachi in the Twenty-First Century

Elements in Music Since 1945

DOI: 10.1017/9781009461320
First published online: June 2024

Donald A. Westbrook
San José State University

Author for correspondence: Donald A. Westbrook, donald.westbrook@sjsu.edu

Abstract: This Element contributes to the interdisciplinary study of mariachi, especially in the United States, by focusing on two areas that have yet to receive substantive academic attention: philanthropy and museum studies. In 2011, UNESCO included mariachi music on its list of expressions of intangible cultural heritage. While it is undoubtedly true that mariachi is in many ways intangible, this downplays expressions of its rich material culture and the work of scholars to research mariachi history beyond an emphasis on musical performance. The first section considers mariachi collecting and philanthropy in the US, especially the efforts of Edward E. Marsh and Chris Strachwitz. The second section examines the first major mariachi history museum/exhibit in the US, managed by the Mariachi Scholarship Foundation and housed at Southwestern College in California. Finally, some open areas for research are proposed and appendices concerning mariachi studies in the US are provided.

Keywords: mariachi, United States, philanthropy, museums, interdisciplinarity

ISBNs: 9781009461337 (HB), 9781009461368 (PB), 9781009461320 (OC)
ISSNs: 2632-7791 (online), 2632-7783 (print)

Contents

¡De la tierra, de la raza, del cielo, de la noche, de la luna, y del sol vengo yo!	*From the land, from the people, from the sky, from the night, from the moon, and from the sun come I!*
¡Soy la voz de mi pueblo, de mis padres, de su alma;	*I am the voice of my homeland, of my ancestors, of your soul;*
Soy la voz antigua, llevo la historia de México y la traigo, de primera luz la traigo al futuro, y hasta el fin de la vida!	*I am the ancient voice, I carry with me the history of Mexico and I bring it, from first light I bring it into the future, and until the end of life!*
¡Soy Mariachi, soy Mariachi, soy la voz de México!	*I am Mariachi, I am Mariachi, I am the voice of Mexico!*

–Introduction from José Hernández and Jeff Nevin's Concerto for Mariachi and Orchestra, "Pasión Mexicana" (Mexican Passion) (Nevin, 2002, p. 241)

Introduction: Mariachi Studies and Making the Intangible Tangible

Academic studies of mariachi have grown in quantity and sophistication, based on contributions from Mexico[1] and the proliferation of English-language scholarship in terms of theses and dissertations[2] and articles, book chapters, and monographs.[3] Generally speaking, and quite understandably, the focus of most of this academic work has been on mariachi as a genre, its history, innovations, styles, musicians, and groups, as well as the ways in which particular cities (and

[1] Examples are Campos, 1928, 1930; Galindo, 1933; Saldívar, 1934; Mendoza, 1956; Garrido, 1974; Rafael, 1983; Urrutia de Vazquez & Saldana, 1984; Jáuregui, 1990; 2001; Betancourt, 1992; Flores y Escalante, 1994; Ochoa, 2000; 2001; 2015; Romero, 2001; Martínez & Clark, 2012; Ku, 2014, 2015, 2016, 2017; Samaniega, 2020; Gómez Arriola, 2020; and Hernandez et al., 2022.

[2] See, e.g., Cashion, 1967; Fogelquist, 1975; Sheehy, 1979; Loza, 1985; Pearlman, 1988; Dodd, 2001, Henriques, 2006; Rodríguez, 2006; Mulholland, 2007a; Salazar, 2011; Ricketts, 2013; Flores, 2015; Fogelquist, 2017; Garibay, 2017; Suarez, 2017; Munguía, 2018; Smith, 2018; Guerra, 2021; Juarez, 2021; and Morgan-Thornton, 2021.

[3] These include, *inter alia*, Stevenson, 1952; Geijerstam, 1976; Gradante, 1982, 2008; Fogelquist, 1996, 2001, 2002; Sheehy, 1997, 1998, 1999, 2002, 2006, 2016; Clark, 2002, 2012, 2021; Nevin, 2002; Pérez, 2002; Rodríguez, 2009, 2010, 2023; Mulholland, 2004, 2007b, 2013, 2021; Gurza, Clark, & Strachwitz, 2012; Madrid, 2013; Howard, Swanson, & Campbell, 2014; Campbell & Flores, 2016; Gaytán & de la Mora, 2016; Flores, 2017; Schmidt & Smith, 2017; Lechuga & Schmidt, 2017; Ulloa, 2019, 2024; Christiansen, 2023; Chappell, 2023; Rodriguez & Ayala, 2023, pp. 70–79.

their festivals, in say Tucson, San Antonio, San Diego, Albuquerque, Rosarito, and Tecalitlán) (Hippler, 1969; Clark, 1980; Fogelquist, 1996, 2002; Rodríguez, 2000) have helped foster its growth and enduring popularity, especially as one form of cultural appreciation and identity for young Mexican-Americans. In fact, many American states, especially in the Southwest, offer mariachi programs at the middle school, high school, and even college/university levels (Monaghan, 2007; Salazar, 2011; NBC News, 2012; Ricketts, 2013; Gradante, 2015; Pedroza, 2017; Guerra, 2021; Ballí, 2022).

Mariachi studies, it can be argued, is an inherently interdisciplinary subfield, and many of its researchers, again not surprisingly, have arisen from music and ethnomusicology departments, especially in the United States. In preparing for this Element, I originally had a more thoroughly historiographical goal: to offer a very brief history of mariachi and then survey some of the ways in which particular players, and especially scholars, have contributed to this growing field. It soon became evident, though, that this goal would be unrealistic in scope and better served by others who are more embedded in this milieu, in particular the numerous *scholar-musicians* (e.g., Mark Fogelquist, Jonathan Clark, Daniel Sheehy, Jeff Nevin, and Russell Rodríguez) who have lived and written about such history, in both English and Spanish. Like many (though certainly not all) American researchers of mariachi, I approach the topic as a non-Hispanic white man who has developed a sustained personal and academic interest in the music and its rich culture and stakeholders. My own training – in philosophy, history, religious studies, and information studies – is likewise interdisciplinary, and I feel that this relatively "outsider" status (i.e., to both the genre and ethnomusicology) positions me to observe and analyze in ways that are perhaps unorthodox yet interdisciplinary and productive for mariachi studies moving forward.

Despite the inherent interdisciplinarity of a field such as ethnomusicology, the academic study of mariachi has ample room to grow as it begins to shift attention away from mariachi history, evolutions, major players, and practices, and toward other subjects. In 2011, UNESCO included mariachi music on its list of expressions of intangible cultural heritage for humanity. While it is undoubtedly true that mariachi is in many ways *intangible*, this downplays some of the ways in which mariachi culture has been expressed as well as the work of mariachi scholars in documenting and preserving this history, not to mention the *tangible* ways in which festivals, secondary schools, and institutions of higher learning support and promote mariachi studies (see, e.g., González, 2015; Hernández et al., 2022).

Huib Schippers (2015) has written powerfully on the connections between applied ethnomusicology, intangible heritage, interdisciplinarity, musical ecosystems, and sustainability. "While many archiving efforts, recording projects, festivals, and even the highly visible *Masterpieces of Intangible Cultural Heritage* initiatives of UNESCO still seem to approach music genres as artifacts rather than organisms," Schippers notes, "there is increasing consensus that a dynamic approach to processes of music sustainability and change is imperative" (2015, p. 136; see also Schippers & Grant, 2016). The question of how, why, when, and who should be involved in making the intangible tangible, documented, preserved, and protected is of course highly political and engenders questions of power, privilege, authority, colonialism, and heteronormativity, among others. In the case of mariachi studies, this is all the more the case because, again, many of the major academic and professional players are white Americans rather than Mexican nationals or Mexican Americans.[4] As Lechuga and Schmidt observed, "People like Jeff Nevin who has offered the first mariachi degree in the world, Mark Fogelquist who has been one of the greatest mariachi educators, and Jonathan Clark, a well-known mariachi historian, are some of the big names in the mariachi world, and they are all White" (2017, p. 89). In a similar vein, Campbell and Flores have observed, "While cultural meaning of mariachi music undoubtedly originates as Mexican, one can find people of all cultures and backgrounds desiring to learn how to play this music, a remarkable number of whom are not of Mexican heritage" (2016, p. 274). Daniel Sheehy explained it as follows in his book *Mariachi Music in America*: ". . . oftentimes over the years, someone from our audience would come up to me and say something such as 'You don't look Mexican.' This simple comment, repeated hundreds of times, along with many insightful, cross-cultural encounters with Mexican musicians, made me acutely aware of the social dimension of mariachi music" (2006, p. 8). "Why, I would ask myself, would audiences not likely tell Chinese cellist Yo-Yo Ma 'You don't look German' when he plays the baroque music of Bach," he asked, "but they would tell me 'You don't look Mexican' when I played mariachi music? What was different? Why was one music so racialized and the other not?" (2006, p. 8). These sorts of ethnomusical, cultural, and sociological realities, and the larger forces involved in what may be regarded as the "Americanization" of mariachi, have been acknowledged by Mexicans, including well-known mariachis, such as Rubén Fuentes (1926–2022) of the famed group Mariachi Vargas de Tecalitlán. When asked in 2008 about the popularity and success of mariachi education programs in the US, Fuentes remarked: "It just makes me sad that here in Mexico we don't copy them." He explained, "When we see how the music is so accepted in the United States, how they have mariachi classes in schools, and they even receive degrees in mariachi, it makes me a little jealous that they haven't done the same thing here [in Mexico]" (Fuentes, 2008).

4 For an excellent discussion of these dynamics of legitimacy, sociology, and identity, especially in relation to Chicanos in recent mariachi music history, see Rodríguez, 2006, pp. 165–87.

This Element aims to contribute to the interdisciplinary studies of mariachi music and culture by giving attention to two areas that have thus far received little academic attention: philanthropy and museum studies. Methodologically, I rely heavily on oral history, ethnography, and archival research. The first section considers the role of mariachi philanthropy through a case study of Edward E. Marsh, an American in Mexico. Marsh is a lifelong mariachi enthusiast and collector who has become a major financial supporter of festivals, educational programs, and arts and culture over the last decade. No previous academic work has given substantial attention to Marsh and his influence, and this section helps fill a lacuna and documents some of the ways in which Mexican and American culture, music, philanthropy, and education have intersected with recent mariachi history. I interviewed Marsh on numerous occasions over the course of three years at his home in Rosarito, Mexico, and this section makes use of highlights from this oral historical data. Marsh is compared and contrasted with another American supporter of Mexican music, the late Chris Strachwitz (1931–2023) of the Arhoolie Foundation. The second section examines the first museum/exhibit in the United States dedicated to mariachi history and culture – curated by scholar-musician Jeff Nevin of the Mariachi Scholarship Foundation and, as of this writing, housed at his academic institution, Southwestern College in Chula Vista, California. This section includes ethnographic observations of the Southwestern College mariachi exhibit based on an extensive tour with Nevin in early 2023. Nevin's role at Southwestern College is introduced, and Southwestern is analyzed as one pioneering force in mariachi studies within higher education. The final section proposes some open areas for research in mariachi studies, particularly topics that would continue to push the interdisciplinary boundaries of this emerging subfield to include even more perspectives, methodologies, and disciplines. I also give historiographical attention to developments in mariachi studies, especially expressions within academia, again with an emphasis on the United States. Finally, three appendices are provided that I hope will serve as resource guides for students and researchers of mariachi: a timeline of mariachi studies and higher education over the last six decades, a chart that lists academic programs within American states (originally created by Jeff Nevin for the Mariachi Scholarship Foundation's exhibit at Southwestern College), and a listing of some relevant archival and digital collections in the United States.

1 Chris Strachwitz, Edward E. Marsh, Collecting, Philanthropy, and Innovation

The academic study of material, organizational, and philanthropic support for mariachi is one area that would benefit from an interdisciplinary perspective and help fill a lacuna in the secondary literature. Although mariachi studies has certainly benefited from the work of collecting and especially philanthropy, as will be explored more in the following section on museum studies, its role and players have yet to be acknowledged or examined in great detail in the scholarly literature. There has been, to be sure, public support for mariachi programs in middle schools, high schools, and universities, as well as governmental and nonprofit sources of support for mariachi and its academic study.

One such example is the nonprofit Arhoolie Foundation, founded by Chris Strachwitz (1931–2023) (Gosling & Simon, 2013; Smithsonian Folkways, 2022; Traub, 2023) (see Figure 1). In partnership with the UCLA Chicano Studies Research Center, the Strachwitz Frontera Collection of Mexican and Mexican American Recordings at UCLA Library works to preserve and digitize holdings, including those related to mariachi (2022). In 2012, UCLA's Chicano Studies Research Center Press published *The Arhoolie Foundation's Strachwitz Frontera Collection of Mexican and Mexican American Recordings* (Gurza, Clark, & Strachwitz, 2012). Strachwitz was also the force behind Arhoolie Records, founded in 1960 and acquired in 2016 by Smithsonian Folkways Recordings (Arhoolie Foundation, 2024). Arhoolie Records released, for instance, the "Mexico's Pioneer Mariachis" albums (see, e.g., Clark, 1992–1998). For many years, Smithsonian Folkways Recordings was directed and curated by Daniel E. Sheehy, a professional

Figure 1 Chris Strachwitz, founder of Arhoolie Records. Photograph by Tom Pich/National Endowment for the Arts. Public domain via Wikimedia Commons.

mariachi musician (Mariachi Los Amigos) and ethnomusicologist who authored *Mariachi Music in America* for Oxford University Press' series on Experiencing Music, Expressing Culture (2006). Sheehy is a past director of Folk & Traditional Arts for the National Endowment for the Arts in the US (Smithsonian Global, n.d.). He was also a recipient, in 2015, of the National Endowment for the Arts' prestigious National Heritage Fellowship (Smithsonian Global, n.d.), an honor previously bestowed upon Natividad "Nati" Cano (1933–2014) of the famed Mariachi los Camperos in 1990 (National Endowment for the Arts, 2023).

Strachwitz, too, received a National Heritage Fellowship, in 2000. The most relevant academic work that acknowledges his collecting and philanthropy, which extended beyond mariachi music, is the aforementioned *The Arhoolie Foundation's Strachwitz Frontera Collection of Mexican and Mexican American Recordings* from 2012. This resource includes a chapter entitled "Chris Strachwitz: The Making of a Music Man in America" (2012, pp. 12–19). Strachwitz's immense contributions as a collector are mentioned elsewhere in the volume. The Frontera Collection at UCLA, we read, for instance, was "compiled over more than half a century by renowned collector Chris Strachwitz" (2012, p. 7). Strachwitz, a German immigrant, came to develop a love and appreciation for all varieties of music, including American and Mexican genres. The chapter on Strachwitz is notable for how its author, journalist Agustín Gurza, writes about the man and his support with an eye toward explaining how and why someone with white (i.e., European) ancestry could become a major supporter of Mexican and Mexican-American music. "Behind Strachwitz's academic accomplishment," Gurza tells us, "there lies the personal story of how a tall, blue-eyed descendent of European nobility came to be the champion of a humble strain of Mexican music ignored by most Americans and disdained by many upper-crust and middle-class Mexicans" (2012, p. 13). "The Strachwitz saga," we read, "is one of fearless immersion in a gritty folk culture that was as foreign to his own upbringing as the Sonoran desert is to the Swiss Alps" (2012, p. 13). His commercial success is presented as a rags-to-riches narrative (with a "humble, homespun business" [2012, p. 19]). Strachwitz is depicted as hardworking and fair in his work at Arhoolie Records, again in a way that refers to his background: "His straight dealing in money matters helped nurture trust among some ethnic artists who were understandably skeptical of a white businessman asking them to sign on the dotted line. But artists also instinctively had faith in his intentions, because he communicated such genuine enthusiasm and respect for their marginalized music" (2012, p. 18).

Strachwitz, however, is primarily understood to be a records professional, collector, and preservationist more than a philanthropist, and his musical interests extend far beyond mariachi.[5] There has been precious little in the academic literature on mariachi philanthropy, aside from treatments of mariachi festivals, concerts, and associated fundraising (see, e.g., Fogelquist, 1996; Rodríguez, 2000; Salazar, 2011). Lilya Wagner (2004) has written about fund-raising and distinguishes between *external* and *internal* culture. "There is the external culture," Wagner notes, "which is exhibited in outward behaviors and traditions that are readily discernible, such as a mariachi band performance." "Internal culture," on the other hand, she argues, "is less evident because it involves the way people think about situations and conceptualize information" (2004, pp. 6–7). Successful fundraising arguably requires one to appreciate both forms of culture, which can also be considered in light of the tangible/intangible binary, and in the process can lead one to adopt an empathetic mindset that appreciates a culture on its own terms.

But what about the role of philanthropy? In the case of mariachi, American Edward E. Marsh (1951–) illustrates how an apparent "outsider" to Mexican culture and music has in recent years become one of its biggest financial and artistic supporters, someone who has worked to apprehend mariachi's internal as well as external cultural expressions. Like Strachwitz, Marsh is white, a "gringo" to Mexicans, but has established a reputation as both a collector and philanthropist, donating millions of US dollars toward concerts, festivals, and mariachi education, in both Mexico and the US. Unlike Strachwitz, who collected widely across genres, Marsh has been far more focused on mariachi. And, unlike Strachwitz, Marsh has received virtually no attention in the academic literature, although his support of mariachi has been documented by journalists (e.g., Durán, 2015; SDSU, 2015; Drake, 2018; Mijares, 2022; Mendoza, 2022) and he is known among professional mariachis due to the concerts he has organized and promoted. These include performances that feature Mariachi Vargas, Mariachi Nuevo Tecalitlán, Mariachi Los Camperos, and the Mariachi Divas (Marsh Library, 2013, 2014; Marsh Productions, 2015; see Figure 2). Marsh's relative invisibility once again speaks to the sense in which mariachi music may be regarded as "marginalized music" (2012, p. 18), as Gurza put it, but also, perhaps, the ways in which Marsh has privileged live musical experiences over self-promotion or concern about recognition in academic circles.

Marsh made his fortune in the real estate industry in the United States before retiring and focusing on other interests, such as collecting science fiction. He has been an active member of the Church of Scientology for over fifty years and is an admirer of the twentieth century "Golden Age of Science Fiction,"

[5] In the 2013 documentary *This Ain't No Mouse Music*, Strachwitz described his organic recording process as follows: "My stuff isn't produced. I just catch it as it is."

Figure 2 Edward E. Marsh, visiting with Rubén Fuentes of Mariachi Vargas, at his home in Mexico City, April 22, 2014. Courtesy of Edward E. Marsh.

which included Scientology founder L. Ron Hubbard (1911–1986). Marsh's private collection of science fiction is extensive and he has donated substantial portions of its holdings, worth millions of US dollars, to his alma mater San Diego State University, which houses them in the eponymous Edward E. Marsh Golden Age of Science Fiction Reading Room (SDSU, 2013; Westbrook, 2022, p. 35). In fact, it was in the context of my own religious studies research that I first crossed paths with Marsh, including visits to his private Marsh Library, in Rosarito, Mexico, where he has been based for many years. When I first visited Marsh in Rosarito, some ten years ago, I was surprised to discover an abundance of mariachi albums, instruments, paintings, and sculptures, in addition to the science fiction and Scientology materials. A hallway in the lower level of his condominium struck me as tantamount to a mariachi house museum, lined with signed album covers and instruments from luminaries of the genre – Rubén Fuentes, José "Pepe" Martínez, Steeven Sandoval, and so many others.

Over the years, through dozens of conversations, formal interviews, and a review of personal and archival documents, I pieced together Marsh's story of how and why he came to love and support mariachi, first as a collector and then as a philanthropist and concert promoter. Marsh's love for Mexico and Mexican culture goes back to childhood. He was born in San Francisco in 1951, grew up in San Diego, and often visited Mexico, especially Rosarito, on family trips. Marsh likes to say that he was practically "hecho en Mexico" (made in Mexico) since his parents went on their honeymoon at the Rosarito Beach Hotel. His evolution from mariachi fan to philanthropist was gradual. It came as the result of friendships and networking with Rosarito politicians and community groups in the early 2010s, especially the Boys & Girls Club of Rosarito. "Rosy Torres, the club president, is a good friend," Marsh explained, "and she works tirelessly for the children, and the club was the first sponsor, along with the Rosarito Beach Hotel, of a mariachi festival even before I became involved." This festival took place in October 2010 and it was there that Marsh met Hugo Torres, then the mayor of Rosarito. "That festival was an amazing creation and inspired me and so many others to action."

Marsh's support of the Boys & Girls Club of Rosarito led to financial support of mariachi events, concerts, and donations of musical instruments to children. In 2013, he sponsored Mariachi Vargas, arguably the world's most well-known and well-respected mariachi group, to perform a concert in Rosarito. The show also featured the Mariachi Divas de Cindy Shea and was billed as "Vargas' First Appearance in Rosarito." Marsh Library (2013) produced a DVD of the event, including footage of its press conference, welcome party, and student workshops.

One of the attendees and guests of honor at this 2013 concert was Gil Sperry, another American mariachi enthusiast (Manna, 2010). Sperry is the author of the books *Mariachi for Gringos* (2006) and *Mariachi for Gringos II* (2011), both of which introduce lay American audiences to the history and culture of mariachi as well as classic songs (with the Spanish lyrics helpfully translated into English). *Mariachi for Gringos II* even includes a section entitled "Interviews with Gringos for Mariachi," featuring Cindy Shea, Jeff Nevin, Mark Fogelquist, and Jonathan Clark, among others (Sperry, 2011, pp. 109–87).

Sperry, it turned out, would significantly influence Marsh, planting the seeds for the latter's more substantial – and innovative – support of mariachi. According to Marsh:

> [Sperry] played a recording for me of the most famous mariachi group [Mariachi Vargas] accompanied by a full symphony orchestra. The music affected me deeply, more than Jimi Hendrix, George Gershwin, Danny Elfman, or even Henry Mancini. I knew and actually felt that my life would never be the same again. I knew I had to experience it myself LIVE. But I figured the experience must be preserved and shared with loved ones and the entire world. After research, I found the only way I could accomplish this dream was to produce it myself. I called the dream "The Big Concert."

Overcome with the grandeur of combining more "traditional" mariachi music with a symphony orchestra set Marsh down a multi-year path. "The idea blossomed as others heard of this and confessed they too shared the dream," as Marsh put it, and he even commissioned a mural, by Rosarito artist David Silvah, that captured his vision for "The Big Concert." Marsh's vision came to life on December 12, 2015, at the Baja California Center in Rosarito, with 5,000 attendees and an additional 500 VIP guests. The orchestra, he said, was "specially composed of hand-picked Mexicans and American professional symphony musicians, all led by the famous Querétaro Philharmonic Orchestra conductor, Maestro José Guadalupe Flores." The "Big Concert" was also intended to foster Mexican–American relations, which "has been suffering for too many years," according to Marsh. He invited everyone he could to the event and posted a YouTube video explaining more about his motivations. In the video, Marsh expressed his admiration for Mariachi Vargas and shared his discovery that the group "plays with a giant symphony orchestra every ten years or so," and that his concert in Rosarito would allow this rarity to be shared with a large audience (Marsh, 2015).[6] "So I want to personally invite you," Marsh went on in the video invitation, "my friends, my American friends, my Mexican friends, to come to this world premiere of *El Gran Concierto del Mariachi*, its performance, as a show, with Mariachi Vargas de Tecalitlán *con orchestra* [with orchestra], handpicked by the best conductor of mariachi orchestras in the world [José Guadalupe Flores] and colorized with fantastic ballet folklórico dancers to accent" (Marsh, 2015).

Marsh's media company, Marsh Productions, recorded the concert and spent considerable time, energy, finance, and staff hours in editing and production (the concert is available on CD, DVD, and Blu-ray) (Marsh Productions, 2015, 2016, 2022a, 2022b; IMDb, 2016). To say the event was a labor of love for Marsh would be an understatement. "It was a thrilling experience to attend and experience 'The Big Concert,' even if I had to produce it myself!" Marsh shared. "And," he confessed, "it was not without costs: a lovely marriage of 14 years, a million and a half bucks, and constant snickers and outrageous price tags from literally every quarter even remotely involved. That's quite a trick when you've never produced a concert before, never produced a music CD or DVD, and can't even speak Spanish!"

Despite the personal and financial costs, the concert's success earned him recognition and respect among mariachis and enthusiasts. Marsh's "Big Concert" later aired on KPBS TV in southern California (2021a) and was

[6] According to Rodríguez (2006, p. 206), Mariachi Vargas performed with the Tucson Symphony at the First Tucson International Mariachi Conference in 1983. In a note, Rodríguez elaborated that "This was not the first time a mariachi performed with a symphony; however, this was the start of a US tradition of mariachi ensembles performing with symphony orchestras" (2006, p. 251).

submitted to the Recording Academy in consideration for Grammy and Latin Grammy Awards (it was not formally nominated, however). Most validating and personally meaningful to Marsh was the praise from mariachi luminary and former Mariachi Vargas director Rubén Fuentes, who attended the concert as his guest of honor. According to Marsh, Fuentes remarked that "this is the greatest mariachi concert of all time."[7] Gabriel Aguilar, formerly director of the Silvestre Vargas Museum in Tecalitlán, echoed this sentiment in a private message to Marsh shared with me: *El Gran Concierto* was, to Aguilar, "the best mariachi concert in the world" and the museum director from Tecalitlán thanked him for a "great gift to the world of mariachi music."[8] Proceeds from the 2015 concert were donated to benefit several charitable causes, such as San Diego State University's Love Library, the Boys & Girls Club of Rosarito, and youth orchestra programs in Baja and Querétaro (SDSU, 2015).

The full 2015 concert is now available online and has gathered over 1.3 million views as of early 2024 (Marsh, 2021b). Marsh has supported other mariachi projects in the intervening years, including concerts and festivals in Rosarito and Tecalitlán. Another highlight for Marsh came in October 2019 with the 10th International Mariachi Festival in Rosarito, which featured a "Mariachi All Stars" lineup that included Pepe Martínez, Jr., Steeven Sandoval, Miguel Angel Barron, Beto Alfaro, Victor Cardenas Garcia ("Pato"), Julio Martínez, Jeff Nevin, and the Ticuán Dance Company, with José Ronstadt (related to the famed Linda Ronstadt)[9] serving as master of ceremonies. The concert made use of an innovative technique that Marsh devised in which mariachis perform live but with a prerecorded symphony orchestra playing in the background and projected on a large screen – a "MagiConcert Virtual Orchestra" (2018; see Video Example 1).[10] This dual technique was also used in an October 2018 concert in Rosarito that benefited the Boys & Girls Club and featured, among others, the Mariachi Divas (Marsh, 2018a) and Trio Ellas (Marsh, 2018b). The well-known Mariachi Nuevo Tecalitlán has also utilized this technique (Canal 4 Zapotlan, 2022). Marsh's vision is that this "MagiConcert Virtual Orchestra" will allow mariachi groups to recreate the sound and experience of his 2015 *El Gran Concierto* (i.e., combining traditional mariachi with a symphony orchestra) but in a way that is convenient and scalable, given the logistics, costs, and venue limitations. Marsh arguably turned out to be ahead of his time, given the manifold

[7] Interview with Edward E. Marsh, Rosarito, Mexico, March 2023.

[8] Personal correspondence from Aguilar to Marsh, December 21, 2020. See also Aguilar (2020).

[9] Linda Ronstadt's seminal album *Canciones de mi Padre* (1987) was influential in the popularization of mariachi music in the US. It was followed by the 1991 album *Mas Canciones.*

[10] The video recording here includes orchestral music for the following mariachi songs: "Maria Linda," "Por Amor," "Bésame Mucho," "Violin Huapango," "Amor y Más Amor (Medley)," and "Qué Bonita es mi Tierra."

possible uses of such a MagiConcert Virtual Orchestra in an increasingly digital age. This is especially true in the wake of the COVID-19 pandemic and the shift toward remote performance on platforms such as Zoom and Webex – not to mention the possible creative uses of such technology in conjunction with artificial intelligence.

Video Example 1 MagiConcert Virtual Orchestra. Courtesy of Marsh Productions.

More recently, Marsh has generously supported the Mariachi Scholarship Foundation in San Diego and their mariachi exhibit at Southwestern College – the first of its kind in the United States – which is analyzed as a case study in the following section. Marsh has also donated generously to the collections and maintenance of the Silvestre Vargas Museum in Tecalitlán (Aguilar, 2020),[11] a modern birthplace of mariachi, and provided instruments to a public school mariachi program in the same Mexican city (Marsh, 2019). Mariachi Vargas' music director, Carlos Martínez, attended the award ceremony at the school and reminded the young, budding mariachi students of the importance of their small city to music history and the world's perception of Mexico and Mexican culture. "I am convinced that from this school will come many future members of the best mariachi in the world," Martínez said to the audience. "Those of you who live here might not fathom the importance of Tecalitlán," he went on. "This is

[11] Gabriel Aguilar, the former director of the Silvestre Vargas Museum, compiled "hundreds of photos" of the museum's restoration and presented them to Marsh in an unpublished volume (Aguilar, 2020). Aguilar included this message on the back cover: "I made a promise to Don Chilo to make a better museum. It was all thanks to Ed Marsh, without his help it would have been almost impossible. Despite the difficulties I had, I did it. Someday I will return to finish my project."

the land of the best mariachi in the world, and Mariachi Vargas de Tecalitlán represents Mexico worldwide. And we honor that responsibility and all our bandmasters. We have had the opportunity to represent you in Switzerland, Japan, Italy, China, all of Europe, South America, Argentina, and many other parts of the world" (Marsh, 2019).

In recognition of his philanthropy and support of mariachi, Marsh received a proclamation from the City of Tecalitlán that referred to him as a "distinguished son" (Marsh, 2019; Sebastian, 2022). In October 2022, Tecalitlán honored him yet again by unveiling a street named in his honor (*Paseo Cultural Edward Marsh*) (Sebastian, 2022). The road intersects with José "Pepe" Martínez Street (named after the famed musician and leader of Mariachi Vargas) in the Town Square. Marsh, like Strachwitz before him, has managed to earn a name for himself as an American supporter of Mexican music and culture. Indeed, American collectors and philanthropists such as Marsh and Strachwitz, as well as American mariachis and scholars such as Nevin, Clark, Sheehy, and others are not merely admirers, supporters, and practitioners but are actively working to *preserve* and *promote* mariachi as a form of art and culture for Mexicans and Americans alike. Their efforts therefore merit even more attention among scholars of mariachi, collections, and philanthropy.

2 Mariachi Scholarship Foundation Exhibit, Southwestern College

The intersection of mariachi studies and museum studies is another example in which scholars of mariachi can expand their disciplinary scope and benefit from analysis beyond the more typical focus on particular groups, performers, styles, and performances. As of 2024, there are only two major museum centers for mariachi in the world: the Silvestre Vargas Museum in Tecalitlán, Mexico, and an exhibit managed by the Mariachi Scholarship Foundation on display at Southwestern College in Chula Vista, California.[12] This section analyzes the mariachi exhibit housed at Southwestern College's library based on a visit and extended tour in early 2023 with curator, educator, and professional mariachi and classical trumpet player Dr. Jeff Nevin. My analysis is based on an approach rooted in museum studies and library and information

[12] Mariachi historian Jonathan Clark, who helped found and curate the Vargas Museum in Tecalitlán in the late 1990s, tells me that there is also an information center related to mariachi history in Cocula, Mexico (Museo de la Cuna Mundial del Mariachi), which, like Tecalitlán, also claims to be an origin point for mariachi. Clark, it should be noted, among many other contributions to mariachi studies over the years, curated an exhibit in San José in 2001 and 2002 at the Mexican Heritage Plaza entitled "A Century of Mariachi Music: The Legacy of Mariachi Vargas de Tecalitlán" (Trevio, 2001).

science (see, e.g., Tucker, 2020) as well as ethnography, participant observation, and oral history (see, e.g., Jorgensen, 1989), including a formal interview conducted with Nevin in his office at Southwestern College that yielded useful background and context.

Nevin's work at Southwestern College is well-known and respected in mariachi circles – among students, academics, and mariachi performers alike (*The Sun*, 2014; Deleon-Torres, 2021). Southwestern College is by no means the only American institution of higher learning to promote mariachi studies and performance. The University of California at Los Angeles, University of Texas Rio Grande Valley,[13] UC Davis, Cal State Los Angeles, Fresno State, Stanford University, San José State University, University of the Pacific, Our Lady of the Lake University (San Antonio), University of Texas at Austin, Texas State University, University of Houston, University of Arizona, and Arizona State University, among others, have offered, and in many cases continue to provide, mariachi related coursework and band options to students. However, as noted in a 2007 article on Nevin in *The Chronicle of Higher Education* entitled "El Profesor de Mariachi," Southwestern College holds the distinction of being the first American college to offer a "degree in mariachi performance, history, and culture" (Monaghan, 2007). According to the Southwestern website, students can pursue an Associate's degree in Music – Mariachi Specialization (Southwestern College, 2023a). This mariachi specialization is described in the academic catalog as follows: "Each mariachi major must declare and take courses on a primary instrument (guitar, vihuela, guitarrón, harp, violin, trumpet, flute, voice), as well as courses on secondary instruments. Includes theory, keyboarding, and sight reading skills" (2023a). Southwestern has its own band, directed by Nevin (Mariachi Garibaldi; YurView, 2022), and student learning outcomes for the specialization emphasize the ability to sing and play music – "including all of the standard mariachi song-types: son jalisciense, huapango, ranchera, bolero, son jarocho and joropo" – as well as the importance of understanding "mariachi history, style and performance practices" (Southwestern College, 2023a). The core course on mariachi history is Music 202, "Development of Mariachi: Style and Culture," taught by Nevin and based on his *Virtuoso Mariachi* (2002) and other resources.

Southwestern's latest contribution to mariachi studies came in July 2022 with the opening of the Ed Marsh Mariachi Museum Exhibit (Mijares, 2022), located on the third (top) floor of the college library. The exhibit, entitled "Mariachi: Historia, Estrellas, Leyendas" (Mariachi: History, Stars,

[13] According to Nevin and Sánchez (2006, p. 13): "the University of Texas at Pan America in Edinburg, Texas (Rio Grande Valley), has long been considered to have one of the top university mariachi ensembles in the country."

Legends), was made possible by support from Marsh, the Mariachi Scholarship Foundation (which Nevin serves as president), and the San Diego Commission for Arts and Culture. A magazine distributed at the grand opening described the exhibit as centered on "the History that breathes life into mariachi: the origin of the word, the evolution of the music, Legends behind the songs, the Stars who presented and enriched the genre, and much more." "The full collection," this same source goes on, "contains several thousand pieces and covers the history of mariachi from the year 1500 to the present day" (San Diego International Mariachi Summit, 2022). Marsh helped finance the exhibit and, in 2021, donated "more than 1,000 LP recordings, 37 bronze and resin busts, numerous historic instruments, *trajes* worn by members of Mariachi Vargas, photographs, artwork, and more" to the Mariachi Scholarship Foundation for display in the museum and study by mariachi researchers (San Diego International Mariachi Summit, 2022; see Figures 3 and 4).

The exhibit's position on the third (top) floor of the Southwestern College Library allows for a nonlinear user experience since it is not immediately obvious to the visitor where the museum space begins or ends. There are advantages and disadvantages to such a design. On the one hand, it integrates the exhibit into the library and allows visitors to experience the sections at their own pace or according to their interests. Also, although the exhibition is open to the general public, many of its visitors will likely be students, staff, and faculty, who may find it more

Figure 3 Marsh touring with Jeff Nevin, curator of the Mariachi Scholarship Foundation museum exhibit, Southwestern College Library, 2022. Courtesy of Edward E. Marsh. Screenshot from YouTube (Marsh, 2022).

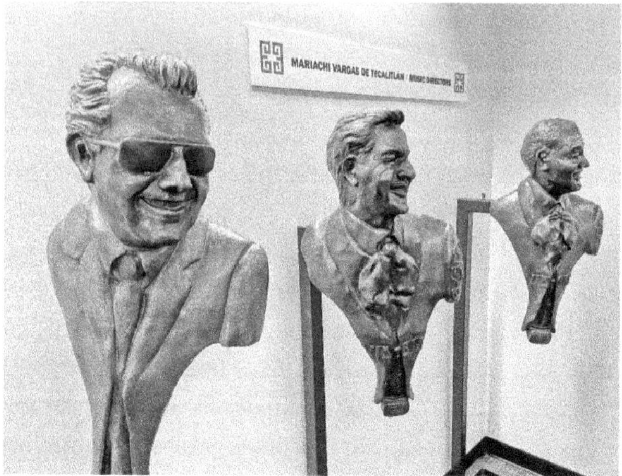

Figure 4 Some of the busts on display, featuring music directors of Mariachi Vargas, Southwestern College Library, March 2023. Photograph by the author.

convenient to peruse the displays between classes or on study breaks, making it an ideal setup for those wishing to appreciate it on multiple visits. On the other hand, the layout may be confusing to a first-time visitor or seem disjointed. This is especially true as one attempts to navigate sections of the exhibit that are spread out along the library's outer walls rather than consolidated in a dedicated room or wing. For visitors not affiliated with Southwestern College, the touring experience may also feel uncomfortable, possibly even intrusive, as one moves between sections near students who use the library for study and research. Another possible problem is that the museum space competes with a more "traditional" library culture at Southwestern. Librarians encouraged those of us on the tour, even Nevin himself in his role as curator at one point, to keep our voices down lest we disturb patrons.[14] Many displays included signs with QR codes that link to audio or video recordings of songs and interviews with mariachis. Unless the visitor saves these QR codes to explore after the tour, the quiet library culture at Southwestern necessitates enjoying these on one's own, presumably with headphones. The most satisfying visitor experience might therefore come from

[14] I have taught graduate courses on historical research methods, library history, and historical museums in the information schools of both San José State University (California) and the University of Texas at Austin. In my course on historical museums, students are introduced to traditional museums (i.e., dedicated buildings, often in urban centers, with ongoing public or private funding) as well as the ways in which museums and exhibit spaces are located in "non-traditional" settings, such as libraries, archives, private or house museums, rural or suburban centers, and, increasingly, digital environments, both corporate and grassroots in origin.

visiting on one's own rather than in a group. In fact, a few hours before my group tour with Nevin, I did just that, exploring ahead of the others to gain familiarity with the space, its layout, content, and flow, and also because it provided the opportunity to take enough photographs for later analysis in a way that would not disrupt Nevin and the tour to come.

All this being said, the exhibit certainly *does* have an intended starting point, marked by a sign in front of the main reference desk on the third (top) floor (see also Mariachi Scholarship Foundation, 2024). This placement serves a wayfinding purpose and invites the visitor to speak with the librarian or staff member for directions in case of confusion. On the back wall behind the reference desk, the visitor to the Marsh Mariachi Museum Exhibit is met with wall signage that introduces the history and purpose of the museum and presents both Marsh, as principal donor, and Nevin, as curator and president of the Mariachi Scholarship Foundation. From this point, the visitor is inclined to move leftward along the wall as the exhibit spaces, including display cases and sculptures, snake along the outer walls of the entire floor. One notable exception is a cluster of display cases near the middle of the floor, behind the main stairway, that impressively showcase a variety of influences on the evolution of modern-day mariachi (e.g., cases to display African, European Renaissance, and Indigenous Mexican era instruments). Notably, signage provides information in both English and Spanish. The bilingual layout makes good linguistic and cultural sense for a mariachi museum, of course, and makes the space even more accessible for Spanish speakers given that Southwestern College (designated a Hispanic-serving institution (HSI) by the US Department of Education; Southwestern College, 2023b) is located in Chula Vista, near the US-Mexico border.

Nevin met with me and two other visitors in March of 2023 for an approximately two-hour tour. With infectious enthusiasm and a deep knowledge of the subject born from decades of experience as a professor and professional musician, he moved us between sections, patiently answered our questions, and introduced us to the basics of mariachi history and culture as well as the rise in academic interest in mariachi, including the role played by Southwestern College. One highlight of the tour came when we were introduced to the myriad meanings of the word mariachi, the subject of one exhibit section. Mariachi, we learned, is not etymologically French, as some have posited, based on the erroneous theory that it derived from the French word for marriage (*mariage*) given the French presence in Mexico and the need for local musicians to play "*mariage* (marriage) music." Although the exact origin of the word mariachi is still unclear, Nevin emphasized the more important point that "mariachi grew out of the combination of Spanish, Indigenous and African music in Mexico" and is a synthesis or amalgam of numerous styles and influences (San Diego International Mariachi Summit, 2022). In appreciation of the diverse cultural meanings of mariachi, our attention was directed to nearby placard subsections with titles such as "'Mariachi' is a Place," "'Mariachi' is a Party," and "'Mariachi' is a Dance."

On another wall, Nevin showed us a display about the *bolero*. This romantic song form originated in Cuba in the late nineteenth century and has become a musical staple for mariachis (see, e.g., Pedelty, 1999). In Spanish, *bolero* is also a term for a "shoeshine boy" and this section of the museum showcases a rare photograph of Rubén Fuentes dressed as a shoeshine worker wearing the classic mariachi *traje charro*. Nevin knew Fuentes and has worked with Mariachi Vargas. Visitors can benefit from this close relationship by accessing QR codes on the wall with numerous resources, including an interview with Fuentes about creating the first bolero ranchero (i.e., bolero in the style of mariachi). The visitor discovers that it came about in the late 1940s during a Musician Union's strike in Mexico City – one in which mariachis continued to work as "they didn't consider us to be musicians," Fuentes recalled to Nevin (San Diego International Mariachi Summit, 2022). As a matter of commercial survival, Fuentes understood that he would need to "teach the mariachis to play romantic music," leading to the creation of the bolero ranchero as it is known today in the mariachi world (San Diego International Mariachi Summit, 2022). This anecdote highlights the marginalization of mariachi and its success in adapting and gaining more popular acceptance as the genre continued to evolve in the twentieth century.

The exhibit highlights mariachi culture as well as the history and evolution of mariachi music and influential musicians. This museological strategy invites the visitor to appreciate how something as intangible or ephemeral as a musical genre can be apprehended and displayed in terms of its material culture, even beyond the displays of instruments and the audiovisual element afforded by QR codes. Elsewhere in the museum, for instance, one discovers, among other items, album covers, paintings, photographs, awards, sculptures of luminaries from Mariachi Vargas, folklórico dresses, and even *trajes* worn by famous mariachi musicians, such as José "Pepe" Martínez (see Figure 5).

We learned that Nevin and the Mariachi Scholarship Foundation have a three-year exhibit agreement with Southwestern College Library (San Diego International Mariachi Summit, 2022). The day after the tour, Nevin and I sat down for an interview that shed even more light on his role at Southwestern, the museum's history, and the future of mariachi studies. He described a path that brought him to the college after graduating with a PhD in music composition

Figure 5 Display cases with *trajes* and personal items of well-known mariachis, including Jorge Negrete and José "Pepe" Martínez, Southwestern College Library, March 2023. Photograph by the author.

from the University of California in San Diego and many years of work as a composer, arranger, conductor, educator, and curator.[15] "I identify as a composer," Nevin told me. "To be honest, I haven't actually composed that much music. I do a ton of arranging," he went on, citing, for instance, impressive work done for Rubén Fuentes and Mariachi Vargas.[16] For many years, he served as conductor of the Southwestern College Symphony Orchestra (Virtuoso Mariachi, 2020a), and for over twenty-five years has played trumpet for the San Diego Symphony. In addition to leading Southwestern's Mariachi Garibaldi, he heads his own mariachi group, Mariachi Champaña Nevin, known for its innovative combinations of mariachi and classical music (Virtuoso Mariachi, 2020b).

In 1998, Southwestern's then-president, Serafin Zasueta, recruited Nevin to teach at the college, head up the mariachi program, and mature it into a degree

[15] Gil Sperry interviewed Nevin, along with a number of other "gringos for mariachi," in preparation for his book *Mariachi for Gringos II* (2011, pp. 109–187), which is recommended for more biographical data.

[16] Nevin also arranged pieces for Marsh's 2015 "El Gran Concierto" (Rosarito), discussed in section 1.

option (Clark, 2005; Mariachi Scholarship Foundation, 2020). "Somebody offered me a job here to start the mariachi program," Nevin remembered in our interview. "The thing that really appealed to me was when he [Zasueta] said he wanted to have a college degree in mariachi music. I said, 'Yes, of course, I'll do that for you.' It was a full-time job to be the first person in the world to create that. That was more interesting to me than being one of 10,000 music theory professors someplace." In addition to spearheading the mariachi degree program, which formally came to fruition in 2004, Nevin has published the textbook *Virtuoso Mariachi* (2002) and numerous bilingual mariachi mastery resource guides and songbooks, tailored for score, violin, trumpet, armonía, guitarrón, harp, viola, and cello/bass (2006, 2016a, 2016b, 2017a, 2017b, 2019).[17] These are used widely in schools, universities, and independent mariachi education programs throughout the US. "I wrote these books that we use in the classroom and that thousands of people have used in their classrooms," Nevin said, waving to copies in his office that he shares with his students. "It is a labor of love."

"The museum came up through Ed [Marsh]," Nevin explained. "I never had the idea that I was going to do a mariachi museum, but he offered this, and I said, I already have all this history that I've been compiling for 20 years that's part of my class. If I could get some funding and actually use that to put this together, maybe we'll have the first or the biggest mariachi history museum [here] at the college." The museum came to life in collaboration with the Mariachi Scholarship Foundation, which received mariachi materials and construction support from Marsh, with Nevin serving as part-time curator. With help from a graphic designer, Nevin worked with the college library to secure the space and prepare the displays and cases. He is already preparing for the museum's future and expansion, intending to relocate the exhibit to a dedicated space in another building. Nevin is cautious about claiming that Southwestern houses the only mariachi museum in the US, since there have been temporary or traveling exhibits over the years and some Mexican restaurants, such as Casa del Sol in Los Angeles (owned by famed mariachi José Hernández), display *trajes* and artifacts (Casa del Sol, 2023). "If I could find the space," Nevin confessed with humility, "I would make it more complete, a museum of the whole history of mariachi," even beyond the exhibit's already extensive efforts to survey major

[17] Nevin's 320-page mariachi "score" volume (2006) is the most substantive and encompassing of these publications (all from the Neil A. Kjos Music Company) and includes pedagogical articles and material to help teach mariachi history along the way. The other, shorter works (80 pages or so each) are "student books [that] contain unique features written specifically for that instrument" (2006, p. 24).

themes and developments in mariachi history over the last 500 years.[18] At one point, Nevin went on, the college "even told me that I shouldn't use the word museum because museum implies a building, whereas this is in the library, so you should use the word exhibit." In the end, the terms museum and exhibit were combined to create the "Ed Marsh Mariachi Museum Exhibit," as it was advertised, with the title "Mariachi: Historia, Estrellas, Leyendas" (Mijares, 2022; GB Magazine, 2022).

During our interview, Nevin recognized the role of American researchers and Mexican American students in mariachi studies, not to mention the ironic influence of the US on Mexico as it slowly begins to mirror American enthusiasm for this expression of Mexican music. In the US, famous mariachi groups such as Mariachi Vargas are regarded as "rock stars," Nevin pointed out. Professional mariachi groups "come to the United States and they treat them better than a lot of the times in Mexico," he continued. "The Mexican folks [who appreciate mariachi] say, 'I can't believe this is happening in the United States. We have to do that here too [i.e., in Mexico].'" "There's a value that a lot of the Mexican Americans place on mariachis that a lot of the Mexican people themselves don't necessarily feel," he went on, and described a nostalgia factor in the US, where the musical form serves as a cultural connection across generations, especially when younger Mexican Americans may no longer speak Spanish yet learn to sing in Spanish in mariachi performance programs. "Imagine the 70-year-old grandma that sees her 15-year-old [grand]kid," Nevin said. "They literally don't speak the same language, but getting dressed up [in *trajes*] and singing the songs, they know the same songs."

As a mariachi scholar and professional musician, Nevin has an eye on the past, present, and future of mariachi. "My personal opinion is that mariachi's going to be evolved more into something like 'classical music,' where there are more and more groups that are going to play songs . . . they're going to keep playing music that has been created over the last hundred years, and that's going to become like a classical tradition." This point is reiterated in Nevin's published work, such as his comparison of mariachi to jazz: "Mariachi music today is at a very similar point in its evolution to that of jazz music in the 1970s. While still generally regarded as purely 'folk' music, many scholars, musicians, students and mariachi enthusiasts have grown to respect the rich and diverse history of mariachi" (Nevin & Sanchez, 2006, p. 11). "Many classical-music composers, as diverse as Aaron Copeland and Silvestre Revueltas," the same

[18] Nevin's observation here points to one of the major drawbacks at the other major museum center in the world, the Silvestre Vargas Museum in Tecalitlán, which focuses on Mariachi Vargas rather than mariachi history more generally.

source goes on, "have drawn upon mariachi music as inspiration ... Clearly mariachi is poised to take its place among the other great classical music of the world" (Nevin & Sanchez, 2006, p. 11; cf. Sheehy, 2006, p. 8). Section 3 considers open areas for research, including evolutions in the genre in relation to "traditional" versus "classical" forms of expression.

As far as the future of the mariachi museum housed at Southwestern is concerned, only time will tell. Still, it enjoys a firm footing thanks to the efforts of the Mariachi Scholarship Foundation and philanthropic support from Marsh and others. Whether the exhibit will remain in the library following its initial three-year commitment remains to be seen. Based on this tour, interview, and observations of Southwestern College, numerous logistical possibilities exist. One is that the museum could stay put and find a permanent home in the library, either in its current location or a more dedicated and private space, which would minimize any possible noise disruptions to library operations. Another is that the museum moves to another building at Southwestern College, such as the new student union building now under construction (Southwestern College, 2023c). Of course, the museum could build relationships with organizations outside Southwestern College but remain in the San Diego area. A partnership might be formed between the Mariachi Scholarship Foundation and, say, the San Diego History Center in Balboa Park or the nearby Chula Vista Heritage Museum.

The museum might also digitize portions of its collection and make them available on a website, hosted independently or within a partner organization such as the Southwestern College Library. This second option would allow Nevin and the Mariachi Scholarship Foundation to utilize expertise in librarianship, digitization, archiving, and preservation and increase access for those who cannot visit in person. One model for a digital collection of mariachi history is Google's online exhibit, "Mariachi, Patrimonio de la Humanidad" ("Mariachi, World Heritage") (Google Arts & Culture, 2023). To its credit, a short video tour of the Southwestern exhibit, featuring Marsh and Nevin (2022), might serve as a basis for expansion or a bridge into a more fully digital experience, if incorporated into a dedicated, separate museum website. The opportunities for digital engagement once again reflect the paradoxes of mariachi and its status as a relatively (in)tangible and marginalized culture. On the one hand, it is nonexistent without its people, places, and physical objects (musicians, instruments, audiences, albums, clothing, etc.) (see, e.g., Conn, 2010) but, on the other hand, it is also increasingly transmissible in digital and intangible forms that can allow for preservation, dissemination, survival, and widespread use.

3 A Survey of Some Open Areas for Research

This final section moves beyond the previous discussion of philanthropy and museums and suggests a number of other open areas for mariachi studies as it continues to move forward into the twenty-first century. In particular, I wish to draw attention to interdisciplinary possibilities that might not be obvious based on the extant English academic literature. In *Virtuoso Mariachi* (2002), for instance, Nevin wrote extensively about a spirit of innovation, change, and experimentation in *mariachi history*, and I believe that this same spirit ought to apply to *mariachi studies* as well. "I dare say that many if not most of the people who scorn mariachis like Mariachi Sol de Mexico for their 'too modern' and 'non-traditional' music – probably the same people who said the same thing about much of Mariachi Vargas' more innovative music years ago," Nevin argued, "would not even know anything of the existence of mariachi were it not – at least indirectly – for these innovative composers, ensembles, and their innovations" (2002, p. 208). "I view the entire history and tradition of the modern mariachi as one which has embraced change," he continued, "and I feel that there is no reason to stop now – there still seems to be quite a bit that can be done" (2002, p. 209). When asked about the future of mariachi, historian Jonathan Clark reflected in an interview that "mariachi music has always been resilient and has been able to successfully adapt to adverse circumstances and situations" (Sperry, 2011, p. 165). "One of the biggest obstacles holding us back," according to Clark, "is a lack of solidarity and conscientiousness on the part of mariachi musicians and groups . . . If we allow our music to become devalued or debased, the whole concept of mariachi education becomes superfluous . . . We need to focus on the bigger picture and work for the greater good of all who play and enjoy this music" (Sperry, 2011, pp. 165–66). In this spirit of humility and collaboration, drawing on this sense of innovation and inevitable change from Nevin as well as respect for mariachi's roots from Clark, I offer the following as a survey of some open areas for future academic research that might benefit from interdisciplinary research methods and foster even more scholarly attention to this subfield.

First of all, the current state of the academic field must be acknowledged, especially since it suggests pathways forward and illustrates the richness of mariachi studies as it has developed in English scholarship from the mid-twentieth century to the present. A number of these essential and seminal works have already been mentioned, such as Daniel E. Sheehy's *Mariachi Music in America* (2006) and the contributions of Jonathan Clark, and I direct readers to the References for a list that is intended to be representative but by no means exhaustive.[19] The last decade, in particular, witnessed a steep rise in the number of mariachi-themed theses and dissertations coming out of American universities, not surprisingly from centers with mariachi academic programming and ensembles.[20] These, in turn, owe a debt of gratitude to earlier pioneers in mariachi studies, such as Mark Fogelquist, whose UCLA thesis (1975) on the contemporary son jaliscience is regarded as a landmark piece that paved the way for others. According to historian Jonathan Clark, Fogelquist's thesis was (and remains) so well respected among mariachi researchers that hundreds of photocopies were made and distributed among English-speaking students and scholars in the years before the rise of the Internet.[21]

UCLA has long been a hub for mariachi research, student groups, and bands, tracing to the early 1960s (see, e.g., Appendix B). Robert M. Stevenson, a longtime UCLA musicology faculty member and advisor, published *Music in Mexico* in 1952 (UCLA Today, 2013). Even before Fogelquist's 1975 thesis, one can find a 1967 thesis from Susan Cashion entitled "The Son and Jarabe: Mestizo Dance Forms of Jalisco, Mexico," which paved the way for her later study and promotion of the Mexican folkloric dance movement (Houston, 2018). In 1974, Daniel Sheehy completed a master's thesis at UCLA on "Speech Deviations as one of the Determinants of Style in the Son Jarocho of Veracruz, Mexico." In 1976, Lawrence (Larry) Saunders completed a dissertation at UCLA on "The Son Huasteco: A Historical, Social, and Analytical Study of a Mexican Regional Folk Genre." Sheehy's dissertation (1979) on the son jarocho deserves special mention, and he, as with Fogelquist, has enjoyed a long career as a professional mariachi and educator. Sheehy would go on to direct the Folk & Traditional Arts program for the National Endowment for the Arts and then the acclaimed Smithsonian Folkways Recordings (Smithsonian Global, n.d.). Fogelquist directed groups such as Mariachi Uclatlán and Mariachi Estrellas de Chula Vista and has taught in numerous mariachi programs. He pioneered a renowned mariachi program at Wenatchee High School (Washington State) and has more recently worked at Chula Vista High School in southern California (with many of his students going on to undergraduate mariachi programs, such as Nevin's at nearby Southwestern College) (Mariachi Spectacular, 2022).

---

[19] My focus here, as elsewhere in this Element, is on English language resources, though many Spanish academic sources are also listed in the References.

[20] Mariachi-themed theses and dissertations have not received substantial attention in the secondary literature. What follows is an abbreviated review of some of the English language materials, found from ProQuest and, in some cases, open access academic databases.

[21] Personal correspondence with Jonathan Clark, May 2023. Sperry refers to Fogelquist's 1975 thesis as a "masterpiece" (2011, p. 143).

In the 1980s, theses and dissertations focused more on mariachi in the United States, reflecting the popularity, influence, and growing appreciation of Mexican music and culture outside its home country. For instance, Steven Loza's UCLA dissertation (1985) analyzed mariachi and other traditions in twentieth century Los Angeles and employed historical and ethnographic methodologies. Loza went on to become a UCLA professor and, in 1993, published *Barrio Rhythm: Mexican American Music in Los Angeles.* A few years after Loza's dissertation, Steven Ray Pearlman, also at UCLA, completed a dissertation (1988) on "Mariachi Music in Los Angeles" that drew on ethnomusicological and anthropological approaches. Output only increased in the early 2000s, with theses and dissertations by Dodd (2001), Henriques (2006), Rodríguez (2006), and Mulholland (2007a), among others. Russell Rodríguez, in particular, has emerged as a significant ethnomusicological voice, authoring numerous mariachi works (see, e.g., 2005, 2009, 2010, 2015, 2023). He now teaches in the music department at the University of California in Santa Cruz (UC Santa Cruz, 2019). Mary-Lee Mulholland, who teaches in the sociology and anthropology department at Mount Royal University in Canada (2023), has similarly emerged as a leading and prolific scholar with several mariachi publications (see, e.g., 2004, 2007b, 2013, 2021).

Production of theses and dissertations in mariachi studies has continued to rise since 2010, with many works coming from second-generation Mexican Americans and mariachis, including a growing number of women as the genre has diversified (Apeles, 2020). These include graduate students who have employed autoethnographic methods or analyzed mariachi history in local or regional terms, including particular states, cities, festivals, and mariachi programs for youth. For instance, Lauryn Salazar (2011) completed an ethnomusicological dissertation at UCLA entitled "From Fiesta to Festival: Mariachi Music in California and the Southwestern United States." Salazar now teaches at Texas Tech University, where she directs the mariachi program and its ensemble Mariachi Los Matadores (Texas Tech University, 2023). She is also a harpist for the Grammy-winning group Mariachi Divas de Cindy Shea (Salazar, 2015, 2023). Two years later, Ricketts' dissertation at Boston University (2013) relied on ethnography and oral historical methods to study mariachi instructors and programs at the K-12 levels in Texas. In 2014, Alexandro Hernández's dissertation at UCLA analyzed the "*son jarocho* and its *fandango* as a migratory and transformative musical culture between nations and social circumstances" (2014), with a focus on Mexico and the US (especially California). In the last decade, increased attention has been paid to race, gender, and sexuality, especially in light of the often patriarchal nature of mariachi groups and culture in Mexico. One notable contribution is Leticia

Soto Flores' UCLA dissertation: "How Musical is Woman?: Performing Gender in Mariachi Music" (2015). In 2017, Mónica Fogelquist, the daughter of Mark Fogelquist, completed a thesis at the University of Texas (Rio Grande Valley) on the subject of "Elevating my Chicana Feminist Consciousness through the United States' First Female Show Mariachi." The younger Fogelquist, who earlier in life played for Mariachi Reyna de Los Angeles, a preeminent all-women group, went on to teach mariachi studies at UT Austin and direct the University of Texas mariachi ensemble there as an assistant professor of practice (Catchings, 2019). Other mariachi-themed theses have emerged in the intervening years (e.g., Garibay, 2017; Liu, 2017; Suarez, 2017; Munguía, 2018; Smith, 2018; Guerra, 2021; Juarez, 2021; Morgan-Thornton, 2021) that likewise forefront issues in gender and race in the mariachi community, both in the US and Mexico.

More recent theses and dissertations offer an excellent window into some of the interdisciplinary research methods beginning to emerge within mariachi studies that make use of ethnomusicology, anthropology, history, and sociology. Based on these trends and trajectories, it seems likely that graduate-level research will only continue to increase, and perhaps we will see material from these theses and dissertations, and others to come, revised and expanded in the form of journal articles, book chapters, and monographs so that they reach even wider audiences. One important academic publication for mariachi research in Mexico is the Spanish-language *Memorias del Coloquio* series associated with El Colegio de Jalisco (2023). However, a new bilingual journal, the *International Journal of Mariachi Education and Performance*, is helping fill a gap by providing a dedicated place for mariachi studies in English and Spanish. Published by the independent Mariachi Education Press,[22] which also produces music guides for performers (2023), the journal's inaugural issue was released in May 2021 and included articles, book reviews, and even reviews of technology and CDs (albums/recordings). The articles cover a wide range of topics and, for the most part, take a pedagogical approach, such as Ramon Rivera's "How to Keep Your Mariachi Students Motivated During Online Learning" (2021, pp. 23–27), Mónica Fogelquist's "The Ingredients for a Successful Mariachi Program in Your School" (2021, pp. 59–64), and Rachel Yvonne Cruz's "Has Mariachi Education Lost Its Mexicanismo?" (2021, pp. 90–97). There is also a section on mariachi history, edited by Jonathan Clark, who authored an in-depth biographical article, "Laura Garciacano Sobrino: California's Archetypical Mariachera" (2021, pp. 103–40).

[22] The first issue (May 2021) included this note regarding publication and ownership: "The journal is currently published by Mariachi Education Press LLC but will soon be published and owned by a nonprofit organization dedicated to mariachi education."

In addition to increased interest in women, gender, sexuality, race, colonialism, student groups, and the "Americanization" of mariachi, which I suspect will continue in the years to come, the scope of mariachi studies might continue to diversify and internationalize. For example, more attention should be paid to the intersection between urban history and mariachi studies, with case studies of particular cities and festivals. One example is a forthcoming study of music in San Antonio (UTSA, 2024), which will include mariachi – all the more appropriate given that the city hosted the first international mariachi conference in 1979 (Clark, 1980). This project is co-sponsored by the University of Texas in San Antonio's library/special collections department and the UTSA Institute of Texan Cultures, and similar to the mariachi museum at Southwestern College, offers an example of how scholars, librarians, and archivists can collaborate in ways that are mutually beneficial across disciplines. Another case in point is the collaboration, mentioned in Section 1, between UCLA's Chicano Studies Research Center and the Arhoolie Foundation (2012). Somewhat along these lines, but more in the sphere of museum and archival studies, the mariachi materials at Smithsonian Folkways Recordings are worthy of more academic attention, given the breadth and depth of their holdings and outreach (such as a magazine, podcasts, videos, and lesson plans) (Smithsonian Folkways, 2024). Moreover, there are now many archival collections in the United States with mariachi materials, which are ripe for research and analysis (see Appendix C, "Selected Archival and Digital Collections"). Beyond attention to particular cities, such as Los Angeles, San José, Albuquerque, San Antonio, Tucson, and Rosarito, among others, researchers ought to also consider the ways in which mariachi is expressed outside of North America entirely. Professional groups such as Mariachi Vargas tour internationally, and the same is true for some student groups, such as Jeff Nevin's Mariachi Garibaldi (Southwestern College), which has performed in Germany, Belgium, Egypt, Russia, and China, among others (Virtuoso Mariachi, 2020c). Indeed, mariachi bands and culture can be found worldwide, such as in Peru, Chile, Colombia, Japan, Croatia, Italy, and Germany (see, e.g., Martínez de la Rosa, 2014; Becerra, 2014; Arias, 2014; Neira, 2014; Corbella, 2015; Malone, 2019; Mulholland, 2021; Christiansen, 2023).

The more familiar fields, such as ethnomusicology and Chicano/a studies, are inherently interdisciplinary, but there are other disciplinary paths for mariachi studies researchers to explore and cultivate. These include, for instance, perceptions and representations of mariachi in popular culture and specifically the relationship between the popularization of mariachi and its depiction in "Golden Age" radio and films, both in Mexico and the US (see, e.g., Mulholland, 2004; Clark, 2005; Henriques, 2011; Toxqui, 2015). While there have been analyses of specific films with mariachi themes, such as Robert Rodriguez's 1991 film *El Mariachi* (Kim, 2013), many more cinematic representations deserve fuller examination, such as the film history of Mariachi Vargas. Another open avenue that could incorporate a media studies approach is a study of English language documentaries on or featuring mariachis. Examples include *Enemies of Silence: The Adventures of Two Travelling Musicians* (BBC, 1991), *Mariachi: The Spirit of Mexico* (2003), *Pasajero: A Journey of Time and Memory* (2004), *¡Viva el Mariachi!* (2004), *Mariachi High* (2012), and *Going Varsity in Mariachi* (2023).[23]

With respect to philanthropy and museum studies, more research ought to be carried out on the role of philanthropists, concert organizers, collectors, and promoters such as Marsh and Strachwitz. This includes museological work related to the Silvestre Vargas Museum in Tecalitlán or the mariachi museum in Cocula. While it may not be possible to pinpoint the exact origins of the word mariachi, a museum studies perspective shifts attention to the manner in which particular groups and towns, such as Tecalitlán and Cocula, appeal to their venerable mariachi roots for the sake of prestige and tourism. Indeed, the intersection of mariachi studies with museum and tourism studies is a natural fit, given how cities, especially in the US, attract tourists to the mariachi economy through concerts and festivals.[24] One of the largest such gatherings takes place annually in San Antonio, which in 2024 will celebrate its 30th annual Mariachi Extravaganza (Camacho, 2023). While the US of course cannot claim to be the birthplace of mariachi, it has devised its own means of diasporic commemoration, such as a "Mariachi Music Hall of Fame" in Albuquerque. Past honorees include Mark Fogelquist, Laura Sobrino, Noberta Fresquez, Rubén Fuentes, José "Pepe" Martínez, Natividad "Nati" Santiago, and Miguel Martínez (Mariachi Spectacular, 2023).[25]

Albuquerque, however, is not the only city with a mariachi hall of fame. Others exist in Tucson, Arizona and Rosarito Beach, Mexico (Drake, 2018; Tucson Internfational Mariachi Conference, 2024), so comparing and contrasting these programs through the lenses of museum studies, cultural studies, and music history might be fruitful. Their existence may also indicate open areas for

[23] A documentary and book project on Tucson's mariachi history, "The Mariachi Miracle," is also in development (Mariachi Miracle, 2022).

[24] For an excellent analysis of mariachi and tourism in Mexico, see Quintero (2015).

[25] Celebration of Mexican music is also discernible in Mexican American historical museums, exhibits, and galleries, even if mariachi is not the primary or exclusive focus. One example is LA Plaza De Cultura y Artes in Los Angeles near Olvera Street, which in 2015 and 2016 hosted an exhibit on mariachi in the area (2023; see also Clark, 2005, p. 231). The LA Plaza museum is a Smithsonian affiliate. The Smithsonian is currently in the process of bringing to life the National Museum of the American Latino, which one can expect to feature music, including mariachi, in the years to come (Smithsonian, 2023).

biographical work on particular musicians and supporters. Another possibility is to view mariachi halls of fame and museums as opportunities to shift attention away from biographical forms of research and toward *organizational* studies that assess the role of institutions and volunteer groups that support such initiatives in the first place. Some of these have already been mentioned, such as the Mariachi Scholarship Foundation, and there are others, including La Frontera Center, the Mariachi and Ballet Folklórico Society, Texas Association of Mariachi Educators (TAME), Mariachi Internaciónal TAMIU, and the Nuestra Cultura Mariachi Association, to name a few.

Mariachi's future as a genre and varieties of its more "traditional" and "classical" expressions should be more fully examined, since these offer entry points into its history, evolution, and innovation. Some mariachi groups, for example, have more conservative views on styles and instruments, such as eschewing the trumpet since it is a twentieth-century addition to the mariachi ensemble (see, e.g., Braojos & Rodríguez, 2004; Los Cenzontles Mexican Arts Center, 2016). Meanwhile, professional mariachis and composers such as Jeff Nevin are pushing the genre forward, with supporters like Marsh advocating for collaborations with classically trained performers and symphony orchestras. Juanita Ulloa, a professional Opera singer and music professor at Chaney College and the California Jazz Conservatory (2023) represents another push toward innovation and mariachi's vocal future within a field traditionally dominated by men. In addition to academic work (2019, 2024), Ulloa has been described as the "High Priestess of Operachi" for her albums and performances that draw on "huapango singing in mariachi style along with boleros and ballads [with] a unique Operachi twist" (Ulloa, 2023). Ulloa also edited a three-volume set of songs and sheet music from Antonio Gomezanda (1894–1961), who, in the late 1920s, wrote the first mariachi opera (*opera ranchera*) (see Ulloa, 2018a, 2018b, 2018c). Decades later, Mariachi Vargas, in a collaboration between José "Pepe" Martínez and Leonard Foglia, unveiled the mariachi opera *Cruzar la Cara de la Luna* (To Cross the Face of the Moon) (Chu, 2023). *Cruzar la Cara de la Luna* is often advertised as the "world's first mariachi opera" (see, e.g., Downing, 2010; Chute, 2013), suggesting that more research should be conducted on the development, composition, and performance of mariachi operas and their reception in and out of Mexico. The intersection of mariachi music and religious culture is another area that deserves fuller examination, especially in light of the genre's use in the Catholic mass (*misa*) (see, e.g., Clark, 2003; Campbell & Flores, 2016, pp. 287–88) and other settings. As Campbell and Flores observed: "Beyond Mexico and Catholicism, mariachi groups have also been invited to perform for religious and cultural ceremonies of the Jewish, Buddhist, and Muslim beliefs. Saint Augustine of Hippo once wrote: 'He who sings, prays twice,' and many have found it in their hearts to sing devotionally with mariachi music" (2016, p. 288).

Mariachi's relationship to material culture and visual (rather than performing) art is yet another possible subject. This might take the shape of focusing on paintings with mariachi themes or perhaps a historical and sociological analysis of charro suits or folklórico dresses. In July 2022, the United States Postal Service began issuing commemorative mariachi stamps (2023), one material and cultural sign that the genre has achieved a level of recognition at the national (i.e., federal) level. "Filled with passion, rhythm, and stories of life, love, and loss," reads the government's description of the new stamps, "mariachi music is an integral element of Mexican American culture that has found fans around the world" (United States Postal Service, 2023). The stamps, designed by Rafael López, are intended to convey the "vibrant spirit of Mexican music" and were inspired in part by the artist's "nostalgic weekends listening to the uniquely Mexican sound of Mariachi music in Plaza Garibaldi in Mexico City" (López, 2022). The 2011 UNESCO designation of mariachi music as a form of intangible cultural heritage, while significant, once again obscures how this genre is bound up within an influential and enduring culture, one that continues to gain recognition and currency, especially in the American diaspora. Items such as American postal stamps serve to forefront and express Mexican culture for larger audiences and in the process raise awareness that perhaps contributes to musical sustainability (see, e.g., Campbell & Flores, 2016).

Most of the interdisciplinary paths described so far presume a reliance on qualitative methodologies, but this need not necessarily be the case. There is ample room for mariachi research projects with quantitative or mixed methods approaches as well. In the field of education, for instance, mariachi programs have been cited in the literature as a positive force in building community, promoting student achievement, and raising retention and graduation rates at the K-12 levels in the US (Crane, 2002; Carranza, 2008; Hillard, 2009; Sperry, 2011, pp. 198–202; Salazar, 2015; Liu, 2017; Smith, 2018). In one study (Kalinec-Craig, 2015), a Texas researcher even investigated the pedagogical benefits of using mariachi to help third-graders learn fractions by framing "equivalent fractions in the context of traditional mariachi arrangements, such as 'Las Mañanitas'" (Chavez, 2016). Another area that might benefit from a quantitative approach is an analysis of the uses of the word mariachi and associated terms in American newspapers and social media, as one way to draw on information, media, or journalistic studies and assess trends in popular culture. A similar approach could be brought to bear on the academic literature, for instance with the use of citation search methods or databases such as Web of Science and ProQuest. This strategy might also be useful in preparation for an annotated bibliography or to develop a literature review on sources available in English, Spanish, and other languages. Another open area for a mixed methods analysis is a study of themes and word uses within mariachi songs themselves, though this would of course require a knowledge of Spanish unless one relies on English translations.

As the academic study of mariachi continues to grow and move both within and beyond its roots in ethnomusicology and performance, interdisciplinary breadth and depth will contribute to its development in the years to come and expose this important subfield to other researchers, in and outside of adjacent fields such as Latin American studies and Chicano(a) studies. In so doing, academic researchers of mariachi and mariachi performers will stand on the shoulders of giants in and out of Mexico, including American musicians, educators, collectors, philanthropists, and festival organizers who have aided in its growth and popularization and who have worked to preserve the tangible and intangible expressions of this dynamic music and its rich cultures.

Appendix A

Selected Timeline of Mariachi Studies and Higher Education Programs in the US, 1960–2024

This timeline focuses on developments in the academic study of mariachi in English as well as its cultural reception, with a focus on the US. It is representative but by no means exhaustive. For example, this timeline does not reflect the rich and complex history of mariachi programs in American elementary, middle, and high schools.

1961: Mariachi student group (Conjunto Uclatlán) begins at UCLA's Institute of Ethnomusicology, spearheaded by graduate student Donald R. "Donn" Borcherdt. Violinist Jesús Sánchez (Don Chuy) is hired to teach a performance class that focuses on three genres: mariachi, son jarocho, and son huasteco. Sanchez would later direct Mariachi Nuevo Calistatlan in the 1970s at California State University, Los Angeles.

1970: UCLA mariachi student group becomes Mariachi Uclatlán ("land of UCLA").

1972: Mark Fogelquist teaches mariachi performance class at San José City College. Rebecca Gonzales is one of the attendees.

1972: Mariachi student group begins at New Mexico Highlands University

1973: El Mariachi Aztlan group formed at California State University, Northridge.

1974: Daniel Sheehy completes MA thesis at UCLA: "Speech Deviations as one of the Determinants of Style in the Son Jarocho of Veracruz, Mexico."

1974: Mariachis play at first graduation ceremony at the University of Texas at San Antonio (UTSA). The band at UTSA is Mariachi Los Paisanos.

1975: Mark Fogelquist completes MA thesis at UCLA: "Rhythm and Form in the Contemporary Son Jaliscience."

1975: David Kilpatrick offers course on "The Music of Mexico" at the University of California, Santa Cruz. One of his students is Laura Sobrino (then Laura Ann García).

1975: Belle San Miguel Ortiz offers mariachi course at San Antonio College (Texas). A mariachi group was associated with the college in the late 1970s and early 1980s. A mariachi program re-emerges beginning in 2017.

1976: Daniel Sheehy establishes Mariachi Nuevo Uclatlán at UCLA.

1976: Lawrence (Larry) Saunders completes dissertation at UCLA: "The Son Huasteco: A Historical, Social, and Analytical Study of a Mexican Regional Folk Genre"

1977: University of Texas at Austin and Texas A&M University–Kingsville (formerly Texas A&I) begin offering mariachi ensemble options to students. The University of Texas band is Mariachi Paredes.

1979: First international mariachi conference in San Antonio, Texas is held, building on the success of Juan and Belle Ortiz's mariachi education school programs.

1979: Daniel Sheehy completes PhD dissertation at UCLA: "The 'Son Jarocho': The History, Style, and Repertory of a Changing Mexican Musical Tradition."

1980: "UCLAtino" first organized at UCLA.

1982: Hermes Rafael publishes *Origen e Historia del Mariachi* (*Origin and History of Mariachi*).

1982: First international mariachi conference in Tucson, Arizona begins, with its first concert the following year.

1983: Annual "¡Viva el Mariachi!" festival first held in Fresno, California, created by the nonprofit organization Radio Bilingüe the preceding year.

1985: Mariachi Ensemble begins at Arizona State University.

1985: Steven Loza completes dissertation at UCLA: "The Musical Life of the Mexican/Chicano People in Los Angeles, 1945–1985: A Study in Maintenance, Change, and Adaptation."

1987: *Canciones de Mi Padre* released by Linda Ronstadt. It will become the best-selling non-English album in US history. Rubén Fuentes served as producer. In 1991, Ronstadt released *Mas Canciones.*

1988: Steven Ray Pearlman completes dissertation at UCLA: "Mariachi Music in Los Angeles."

1989: Nati Cano of Mariachi los Camperos begins teaching a course on "The Music of Mexico" at UCLA. Jesús "Chuy" Guzmán would later continue to offer the course.

1989: Patricia Harpole and Mark Fogelquist publish *Los Mariachis! An Introduction to Mexican Mariachi Music*, with instructional CD, performed by El Mariachi Uclatlan.

1989: Dahlia Guerra begins a mariachi program at University of Texas, Pan American (now University of Texas Rio Grande Valley). Guerra founded Mariachi Aztlán and UTRGV now sponsors the FESTIBA Mariachi Festival.

1990: Jesús Jáuregui publishes *El Mariachi: Símbolo Musical de Mexico* (*Mariachi: Musical Symbol of Mexico*).

1990: Nati Cano receives National Heritage Fellowship from National Endowment for the Arts.

1990: Mariachi USA festival first held in Los Angeles at the Hollywood Bowl.

1990: Mariachi Spectacular founded in Albuquerque.

1991: San José Mexican heritage and mariachi festival first held, with support from the Mexican Heritage Center.

1992–1999: San José State University Mariachi Workshop, led by Jonathan Clark.

1993: Steven Loza publishes *Barrio Rhythm: Mexican American Music in Los Angeles* (University of Illinois Press).

1993: Mariachi program founded at the University of Arizona.

1994: Los Cenzontles Mexican Arts Center is incorporated (based on a youth group founded in 1990).

1994: Las Cruces International Mariachi conference first held.

1994: Mariachi Cardenal de Stanford formed at Stanford University.

1995: Mariachi Vargas Extravaganza founded in San Antonio, Texas by Cynthia Muñoz. This group holds annual mariachi competitions and summer camps.

1996: Palo Alto College (San Antonio) formally launches mariachi program. The student group then is Mariachi Palomino. The current group is the Palo Alto College Marching Mariachis.

1997: Inauguration of the world's first mariachi museum, the Museo Silvestre Vargas, in Tecalitlán, Jalisco, Mexico. Mariachi historian Jonathan Clark is a co-founder and curator of the original exhibit.

1997: Jonathan Clark receives grant from National Academy for Recording Arts & Sciences to transcribe and annotate *sones* by Mariachi Vargas.

1997: University of New Mexico offers mariachi ensemble option to students.

1997: Texas State University (San Marcos) begins offering class for Mariachi Nueva Generación (MNG) in the fall term.

1997: University of Texas (Brownsville) and Texas Southmost College begin Mariachi Alacran which the following year becomes Mariachi Escorpión.

1998: Mariachi Scholarship Foundation (MSF) formally founded, based on the work of Bob Griego, President of Sweetwater Union High School District Board of Directors in California. MSF awards scholarships to high school and college students and later sponsors an international mariachi summit in San Diego.

1998: Jeff Nevin recruited to Southwestern College in Chula Vista, California, to begin a mariachi program. In 2004, Southwestern became the first US college to offer a degree program/mariachi specialization.

1999: Cindy Shea founded Mariachi Divas, which later becomes the official mariachi ensemble of Disneyland.

September 1999: University mariachi band founded at Texas A&M University International (Laredo). The current program is Mariachi Internaciónal TAMIU.

2000: Southwest Texas State University (now Texas State University) Mariachi Festival ("Feria del Mariachi") first held.

2001: Mariachi Véritas group founded at Harvard University.

2001: Dodd completes MA thesis at University of Houston, Clear Lake: "Playing Mariachi Music: Its Influence in Students' Lives, An Ethnographic Study of Mariachi MECA."

2001–2002: "A Century of Mariachi Music: The Legacy of Mariachi Vargas de Tecalitlán" exhibit, Mexican Heritage Plaza, San José, California, curated by Jonathan Clark.

2002: Jeff Nevin publishes *Virtuoso Mariachi* with University Press of America.

2002: Students found Aggieland Mariachi (also known as Mariachi Anillos de Oro) at Texas A&M University in College Station. The group gained university recognition in 2012.

2003: PBS documentary *Mariachi: the Spirit of Mexico* released.

2003: Mariachi Águilda de UNT founded the University of North Texas (Denton).

2004: Southwestern College begins offering an Associate's degree in Music–Mariachi Specialization – the first college in the US to do so.

2004: *¡Viva el Mariachi!* documentary released.

2005: Our Lady of the Lake University (San Antonio) begins offering BA in Music with an emphasis option in mariachi performance and pedagogy.

2005: Mariachi de Brown established at Brown University.

2005: Mariachi Serrano de Claremont formed at the Claremont Colleges in California.

2006: Daniel Sheehy publishes *Mariachi Music in America* with Oxford University Press.

2006: Jeff Nevin publishes *Mariachi Mastery* guide with the Neil A. Kjos Music Company, followed by others in the years to come.

2006: Henriques completes dissertation at UT Austin: "Performing Nationalism: Mariachi, Media and the Transformation of a Tradition (1920–1942)."

2006: Russell Rodríguez completes dissertation at University of California, Santa Cruz: "Cultural Production, Legitimation, and the Politics of Aesthetics: Mariachi Transmission, Practice, and Performance In the United States."

2006: Gil Sperry publishes *Mariachi for Gringos: Unlocking the Secrets of Mexico's Macho Music*. In 2011, a second volume, *Mariachi for Gringos II: Discovering More of Mexico's Hottest Songs and Stories*, is published.

2006: Mariachi ensemble formed at the University of California at Riverside.

2007: Mary-Lee Mulholland completes dissertation at York University (Canada): "Mariachi in Excess: Performing Race, Gender, Sexuality, and Regionalism in Jalisco, Mexico"

2007: University Interscholastic League (UIL) in Texas begins a regional contest for mariachi. In 2016, the first UIL state-wide competition began.

2008: First volume of *Foundations of Mariachi Education*, edited by William Gradante, released.

2008: Mariachi program founded under John A. Siqueiros at the University of Texas at El Paso (UTEP) with the Mariachi Los Mineros.

2008: Mariachi Águila de Oro founded at California State University (Los Angeles).

2009: Mariachi Divas de Cindy Shea becomes first all-female mariachi band nominated for a Grammy (which it wins). The band serves as the official mariachi group for Disneyland.

2010: Jonathan Clark, mariachi historian and pioneer, hired as mariachi program director at Stanford University.

2010: Mariachi Los Matadores founded at Texas Tech University in Lubbock.

2011: Lauryn Salazar completes dissertation at UCLA: "From Fiesta to Festival: Mariachi Music in California and the Southwestern United States."

2011: Mariachi music ("Mariachi, string music, song and trumpet") recognized by UNESCO as intangible cultural heritage for humanity.

2012: Agustín Gurza, with Johnathan Clark and Chris Strachwitz, publishes *The Arhoolie Foundation's Strachwitz Frontera Collection of Mexican and Mexican American Recordings* (UCLA Chicano Studies Research Center Press).

2012: Mariachi Luz de Oro founded at the University of California at Berkeley.

2012: Mariachi ensemble formed at University of San Diego. The university also hosts an annual mariachi conference, dating to 2006.

Fall 2012: Mariachi group founded at San Diego State University under Mark Fogelquist.

2013: Jonathan Clark receives Vicente T. Mendoza Award from the Mexican government in recognition of his contributions to a greater understanding of mariachi music, history, and culture.

2013: Ricketts completes dissertation at Boston University: "Mariachi as a Music Education Genre: A Study of Program Status, Pedagogical Practices, and Activities."

2013: Mariachi Cielito Lindo formed at University of California, Davis.

2013: Mariachi Los Correcaminos founded at Metropolitan State University of Denver.

2013: Mariachi Son de Esperanza formed at Texas A&M University (San Antonio). This group later disbanded and, as of 2022, the official group at the university is Mariachi Los Jaguares del Sur.

October 2013: Mariachi Luna Llena recognized as an organization at Rice University in Texas.

2014: International Women's Mariachi Festival first held in Los Angeles.

2014: Alexandro David Hernández completes dissertation at UCLA: "The *Son Jarocho* and *Fandango* Amidst Struggle and Social Movements: Migratory Transformation and Reinterpretation of the *Son Jarocho* in La Nueva España, México, and the United States."

2014: Mariachi Fuego founded at the University of Illinois (Chicago).

2015: Leticia Soto Flores completes dissertation at UCLA: "How Musical is Woman?: Performing Gender in Mariachi Music."

2015: Daniel Sheehy receives National Heritage Fellowship from National Endowment for the Arts.

2015–2016: Mariachi exhibit at LA Plaza de Cultura y Artes in Los Angeles.

2016: Robin Sacolick completes dissertation at UC Santa Cruz: "Transcendence and *Son Jarocho* as Practiced in the San Francisco Bay Area."

2016: Mariachi Los Caballeros founded at Cal Poly Pomona.

2016: Mariachi Plata founded at Western New Mexico University.

2017: Monica A. Fogelquist completes master's thesis at University of Texas, Rio Grande Valley: "Elevating my Chicana Feminist Consciousness through the United States' First Female Show Mariachi."

2017: Garibay completes master's report at California State University, Long Beach: "Towards a Hybrid Approach to Mariachi Education: Bridging the Gap between Formal and Informal Transmission of Musical Culture."

2017: Suarez completes MA graduate project at California State University, Northridge: "Fina Estampa: A Musical Journey Through Mexico."

2017: FangYuan Liu completes Master of Music thesis at the University of Arizona: "The Impact of Mariachi Education on Academic Achievement in Tucson High Magnet School and Pueblo Magnet High School."

2018: Munguía completes MA thesis at California State University, Northridge: "The Impact of Mariachi Instructional Programs on the Son de Mariachi among Student Mariachi Ensembles."

2018: Smith completes master's thesis at University of the Pacific: "The Influences of a Mariachi Education on Student Perceptions of Academic Achievement, Academic Attainment, and Student Engagement."

2018: University of Texas (Rio Grande Valley) begins offering an undergraduate mariachi concentration at its School of Music.

2018: Mariachi Oroazul founded at San José State University.

2019: Monica Fogelquist becomes professor of practice and pioneers a mariachi program at UT Austin. In 2020, Fogelquist teaches "History of Mariachi Music."

2019: Mariachi Women's Foundation incorporated in Los Angeles by Leonor X. Perez.

2019: Mariachi Pumas founded at the University of Houston.

2019: Mariachi Osos del Valle formed at Phoenix College.

2019: Mariachi Ocelotlán founded the University of the Pacific.

2019: Mariachi Plata founded at College of Southern Nevada, building on the success of a mariachi course first offered in 2015.

2021: Clyde M. Guerra completes master's thesis at University of Texas, Rio Grande Valley: "Mariachi Programs at the University Level: Investigating Eurocentric Stereotypes."

2021: Juarez completes MA thesis at California State University, Los Angeles: "Las Mariachis Suenan: How Mariachi Womyn are Challenging Gender Norms through their Collective Experiences."

2021: Morgan-Thornton completes Doctor of Music Education thesis at Liberty University: "Analysis of Texas Collegiate Mariachi Ensembles: Standard Repertoire and Genres."

May 2021: First issue of the *International Journal of Mariachi Education and Performance* released by the Mariachi Education Press.

July 2022: Ed Marsh Mariachi Museum Exhibit opens at Southwestern College Library, curated by Jeff Nevin and sponsored by the Mariachi Scholarship Foundation.

July 2022: United States Postal Service releases mariachi stamps, designed by Rafael López.

August 2022: Mariachi program relaunches at Pima College in Arizona.

2023: Release of documentary *Going Varsity in Mariachi*, which premieres at Sundance Film Festival.

2023: National Recording Registry of the Library of Congress inducts "The Very First Mariachi Recordings."

June 15, 2023: Mariachi Vargas performs at the White House, building on a growing tradition of mariachi performances for US governmental officials.

2024: Juanita Ulloa publishes *The Mariachi Voice* with Oxford University Press.

Appendix B

Chart of Mariachi Programs in American Higher Education, 1960–2022

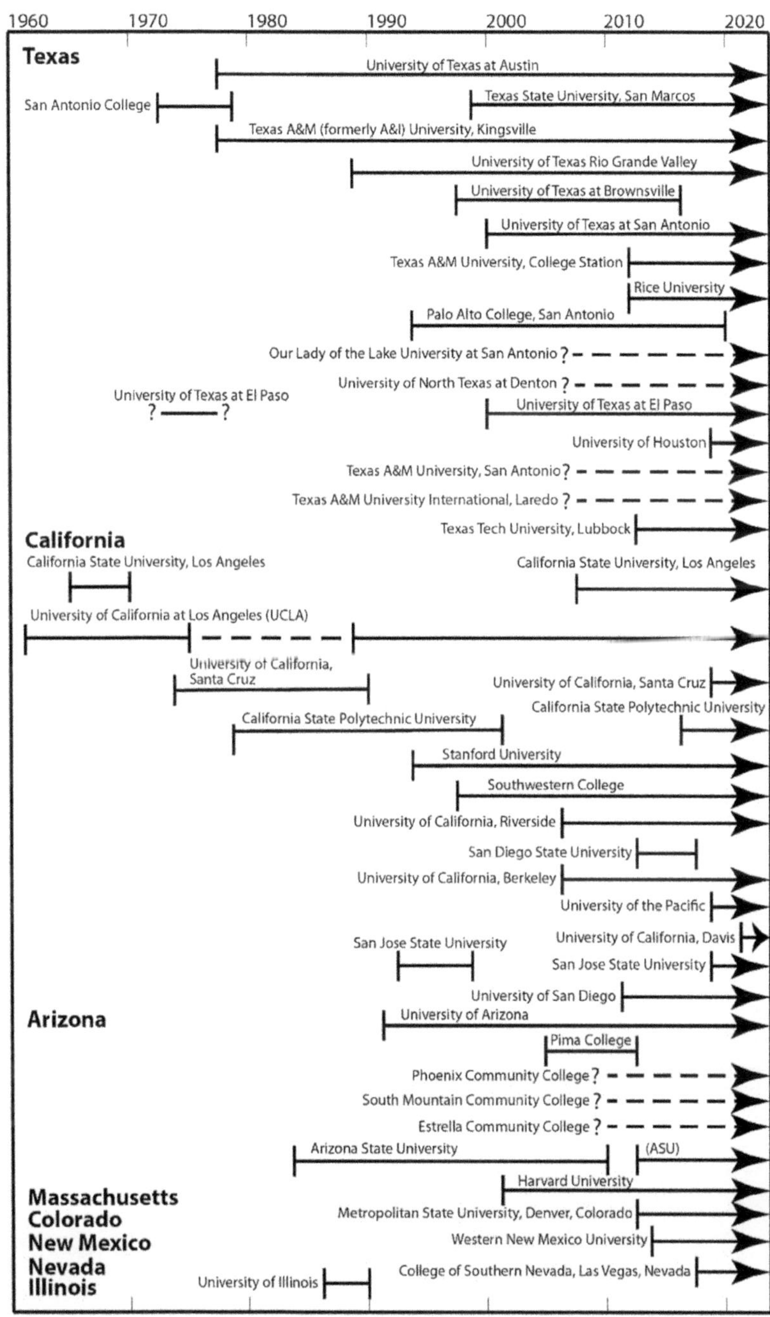

This chart is reproduced courtesy of its creator, Jeff Nevin, President of the Mariachi Scholarship Foundation and Professor of Music and Director of Mariachi Activities at Southwestern College. A copy is on display at the foundation's mariachi history exhibit.

Appendix C

Selected Archival and Digital Collections

Chicano Studies Research Center, UCLA: https://www.chicano.ucla.edu/library/holdings

Chris Strachwitz Collection, UCLA: https://oac.cdlib.org/findaid/ark:/13030/c8s188w0/?query=mariachi

Donn Borcherdt Collection, 1960–1966, UCLA Ethnomusicology Archive: https://oac.cdlib.org/findaid/ark:/13030/kt0t1nc989/?query=mariachi and https://digital.library.ucla.edu/catalog/ark:/21198/zz002jn50n

El Centro Chicano, Stanford University: https://oac.cdlib.org/findaid/ark:/13030/kt8n39s233/?query=mariachi

Internet Archive, "Mariachi" items: https://archive.org/search?query=mariachi

Mariachi Spectacular Records (MSS 521), Center for Southwest Research and Special Collections, University of New Mexico Libraries. https://nmarchives.unm.edu/repositories/22/resources/1700

Smithsonian Folkways Recordings, https://folkways.si.edu/

Strachwitz Frontera Collection of Mexican and Mexican-American Recordings, UCLA: https://frontera.library.ucla.edu/

References

Aguilar, G. (2020). *Restoration of the Silvestre Vargas Museum*. Volume of photographs compiled by Gabriel Aguilar, museum director, 2018–2019. Unpublished; in private collection of Edward E. Marsh.

Albuquerque Historical Society. (2023). "History of Mariachi in Albuquerque." Presentation by Peter Sanchez. Posted to YouTube, March 19. www.youtube .com/watch?v=7U70e0ivzpI&t=4s.

Apeles, T. (2020). "The Rise of the Female Mariachi: A Brief History." *KCET*, July 29. www.kcet.org/shows/southland-sessions/the-rise-of-the-female-mariachi-a-brief-history.

Arhoolie Foundation. (2024). About the Arhoolie Foundation. https://arhoolie .org/about-us/.

Arias, L. O. M. (2014). "El mariachi en Chile." In L. Ku, ed., *El Mariachi: Aprendizajes y Relaciones*, 243–57. Zapopan: El Colegio de Jalisco.

Ballard, K. R., & C. R. Benavidez. (2002). "Mariachi: Ethnic Music as a Teaching Tool." *Teaching Music*, *9*(4), 22–27.

Ballí, C. (2022). "A Championship Season in Mariachi Country." *The New York Times*, November 3. www.nytimes.com/2022/11/03/magazine/mariachi-texas .htm.

BBC. (1991). *Enemies of Silence: The Adventures of Two Travelling Musicians*. Documentary directed by Jeremy Marre. London.

Becerra, J. A. C. (2014). "Bailamos el mismo son: Representaciones pictóricas de las danzas populares en México y Chile." In L. Ku, ed., *El Mariachi: Aprendizajes y Relaciones*, 231–42. Zapopan: El Colegio de Jalisco.

Betancourt, I. G. (1992). "Mariachi: En Busca del Étimo Perdido." *Estudios Jaliscienses*, *9*, 36–52. www.estudiosjaliscienses.com/1992/08/01 /num-9/.

Braojos, R. & E. Rodríguez (dirs.) (2004). *Pasajero: A Journey of Time and Memory*. San Pablo: Los Cenzontles Mexican Arts Center.

Brown, P. L. (2005). "Sousa? Many Students March to Mariachi Instead?" *The New York Times*, April 24. www.nytimes.com/2005/04/24/us/sousa-many-students-march-to-mariachi-instead.html.

California's Gold. (1993). "Mariachi." Episode 406. Video Archived at Chapman University, Huell Howser California's Gold Archive, December 10. https://blogs.chapman.edu/huell-howser-archives/1993/12/10/mariachi-californias-gold-406/.

Camacho, L. (2023). "NEW DATE for the 29th Annual Mariachi Extravaganza is Announced!" *MariachiMusic.com*, March 16. https://mariachimusic.com/blog/2023/03/new-date-for-the-29th-annual-mariachi-extravaganza/.

Campbell, P. S., & L. S. Flores. (2016). "Mariachi Music: Pathways to Expressing Mexican Musical Identity." In H. Schippers & C. Grant, eds., *Sustainable Futures for Music Cultures: An Ecological Perspective*, 271–302. New York: Oxford University Press.

Campos, R. M. (1928). *El Folklore y La Música Mexicana: Investigación Acerca De La Cultura Musical en México (1525–1925)*. México: Publicaciones de la Secretaría de Educación Pública.

Campos, R. M. (1930). *El Folklore Musical de Las Ciudades*. México: Secretaría de Educación Pública.

Canal 4 Zapotlan. (2022). "Magiconcert Mariachi Nuevo Tecalitlán." Posted to Canal 4 Zapotlan's Facebook page, January 7. www.facebook.com/Canal4Zapotlan/videos/339850141063478/.

Carranza, R. (2008). "Mariachi Instruction in Support of Literacy." In W. Gradante, ed., *Foundations of Mariachi Education: Materials, Methods, and Resources*, 167–74 . Vol. 1. Lanham, MD: Rowman and Littlefield.

Casa del Sol. (2023). Homepage. www.casadelsoloc.com/.

Cashion, S. V. (1967). "The Son and Jarabe: Mestizo Dance Forms of Jalisco, México." MA thesis. University of California, Los Angeles.

Catchings, J. (2019). "Professor Mónica Fogelquist Takes the Lead of the University of Texas Mariachi Ensemble." Butler School of Music. University of Texas, Austin, October 23. https://music.utexas.edu/news/professor-monica-fogelquist-takes-lead-university-texas-mariachi-ensemble.

Los Cenzontles Mexican Arts Center. (2016). "Mariachi Tradicional." www.loscenzontles.com/mariachi-tradicional/.

Chappell, E. (2023). "The Life and Career of Mariachi Educator Zeke Castro." *Journal of Historical Research in Music Education*. https://doi.org/10.1177/15366006231185561.

Chavez, J. (2016). "Can Mariachi Music Be Used to Teach Mathematics to Third Graders?" *UTSA Today*, January 13. www.utsa.edu/today/2016/01/mariachimath.html.

Chavira-Prado, A. (2022). *Mucho Corazón: Stages in the Life of a Pioneer Female Mariachi*. New York: Peter Lang.

Christiansen, M. S. (2023). "Building Identity and Authenticity: Exploring the Spatiotemporal Aspects of Language Teaching in a Mariachi Class." *International Journal of Bilingual Education and Bilingualism*, *27*(2), 201–12.

Chu, J. (2023). "A Mariachi Opera? How Two Art Forms Combined to Celebrate the Immigrant Story." *Smithsonian Center for Folklife and Cultural Heritage*

Magazine, April 12. https://folklife.si.edu/magazine/mariachi-opera-immigrant-story.

Chute, J. (2013). "SD Opera Presents First Mariachi Opera." *The San Diego Union-Tribune*, March 13. www.sandiegouniontribune.com/entertainment/classical-music/sdut-san-dieg-opera-mariachi-2013mar13-htmlstory.html.

Clark, J. (1980). "Report: First International Mariachi Conference, San Antonio, Texas, September 27–30, 1979." *ANGF Journal*, *4*(1), 21–23.

Clark, J. (1992–1998). Liner notes, *Mexico's Pioneer Mariachis*, Vol. 1–4, Folklyric CD 7011, 7012, 7015, and 7036. El Cerrito: Arhoolie Productions.

Clark, J. (1996). "Mariachi." In *The Latino Encyclopedia*. New York: Marshall Cavendish. https://web.archive.org/web/20231210134742/https://www.sobrino.net/mer/entry_on_the_word_mariachi.htm.

Clark, J. (ed.) (2002). *Sones from Jalisco as Played by the World's Greatest Mariachi: Transcriptions Authorized by Rubén Fuentes and Revised by Members of Mariachi Vargas de Tecalitlán*. 10 Vols. San José: San José State University Mariachi Workshop.

Clark, J. (2003). 'Mariachi Group,' '*Guitarrón*,' and '*Vihuela*.' In J. Shepherd, P. Oliver, P. Wicke, D. Horn, & D. Laing, eds., *Continuum Encyclopedia of Popular Music of the World*, Vol. 2, 42–3, 426, 452. London: Continuum.

Clark, S. (2005). "Mariachi Music as a Symbol of Mexican Culture in the United States." *International Journal of Music Education*, *23*(3), 227–37.

Clark, J. (2012). "El Mariachi: From Rustic Roots to Golden Era." In A. Gurza, with J. Clark & C. Strachwitz eds., *The Arhoolie Foundation's Strachwitz Frontera Collection of Mexican and Mexican American Recordings*, 109–26. Los Angeles: UCLA Chicano Studies Research Center.

Clark, J. (2016–present). Articles on *MariachiMusic.com*. https://mariachimusic.com/blog/author/mariachero/.

Clark, J. (2021). "Laura Garciacano Sobrino: California's Archetypal Mariachera." English and Spanish versions provided. *International Journal of Mariachi Education and Performance*, *1*(1), 103–40.

Conn, S. (2010). *Do Museums Still Need Objects?* Philadelphia: University of Pennsylvania Press.

Conner, R. (2011). "Institutional Histories Entry: Ethnomusicology at the University of California, Los Angeles." *The Society for Ethnomusicology*, December 5. www.ethnomusicology.org/page/HS_InsUCLA.

Corbella, A. T. (2015). "El mariachi en Europa: Historia, desarrollo y perspectivas." In L. Ku, ed., *El Mariachi: Regiones e Identidades*, 273–82. Zapopan: El Colegio de Jalisco.

Crane, E. (2002). "Mariachi Magic: This District Is Keeping Its Large Hispanic Student Population in School and Interested with a Different Type of Music Program." *District Administration*, *38*(10), 22–23.

Cruz, R. V. (2017). *The Art of Mariachi: A Curriculum Guide*. San Antonio: Conocimientos Press.

Cruz, R. Y. (2021). "Has Mariachi Education Lost Its Mexicanismo?" *International Journal of Mariachi Education and Performance*, *1*(May), 90–97. Mariachi Education Press.

Deleon-Torres, A. (2021). "Someone San Diego Should Know: Jeff Nevin." *The San Diego Union-Tribune*, January 8.www.sandiegouniontribune.com/lifestyle/people/story/2021-01-08/someone-san-diego-should-know-jeff-nevin.

Dell'Orto, G. (2021). "Mariachi Mass Returns to Tucson Cathedral after a Year of Pandemic Silence." *America: The Jesuit Review*, August 23. www.americamagazine.org/faith/2021/08/23/mariachi-mass-covid-arizona-241271.

Dickey, D. W. (2016). "Mariachi Music." *Handbook of Texas*, published online by the Texas State Historical Association. www.tshaonline.org/handbook/entries/mariachi-music.

Dodd, J. (2001). "Playing Mariachi Music: Its Influence in Students' Lives, an Ethnographic Study of Mariachi MECA." MA thesis. University of Houston, Clear Lake.

Downing, M. (2010). "HGO Presents the World's First Mariachi Opera." *Houston Press*, October 20. www.houstonpress.com/arts/hgo-presents-the-worlds-first-ever-mariachi-opera-6364033.

Drake, R. (2018). "The Rosarito Mariachi Fest Is Here." *Gringo Gazette* (North), October 1. https://web.archive.org/web/20240110170051/https://ggnorth.com/2018/10/the-rosarito-mariachi-fest-is-here/.

Durán, A. (2015). "El Gran Concierto de mariachi se presenta en Rosarito." *The San Diego Union-Tribune*, December 6. www.sandiegouniontribune.com/en-espanol/sdhoy-el-gran-concierto-de-mariachi-se-presenta-en-2015dec06-story.html.

El Colegio de Jalisco. (2023). "Publicaciones." www.coljal.mx/publicaciones/.

Escalante, J. A. C. (2006). *Mariachi Antiguo, Jarabe y Son: Símbolos Compartidos y Tradición Musical En Las Identidades Jaliscienses*. Guadalajara: Secretaría De Cultura Gobierno Del Estado De Jalisco. https://sc.jalisco.gob.mx/sites/sc.jalisco.gob.mx/files/12mariachiajys.pdf.

Flores, L. I. S. (2012). "Performative Metaphors: The 'Doing' of Image by Women in Mariachi Music." UCLA Center for the Study of Women. *CSW Update Newsletter*. https://escholarship.org/uc/item/8pr2x039.

Flores, L. I. S. (2014). "La enseñanza de la música de mariachi en diversos contextos educativos." In L. Ku, ed., *El Mariachi: Aprendizajes y Relaciones*, 311–24. Zapopan: El Colegio de Jalisco.

Flores, L. S. (2015). "How Musical Is Woman? Performing Gender in Mariachi Music." PhD dissertation. University of California, Los Angeles.

Flores, C. R. (2017). "Women Pioneers of Mariachi: Barbara Perez-Díaz y Rebeca Gonzales." *Karpa*, *10*. Los Angeles: California State University.

Flores y Escalante, J., & D. Herrera. (1994). *Cirilo Marmolejo: Historia del Mariachi en la Ciudad de México*. Asociación Mexicana de Estudios Fonográficos: Dirección General de Culturas Populares.

Fogelquist, M. (1975). "Rhythm and Form in the Contemporary Son Jaliscience." MA thesis. University of California, Los Angeles.

Fogelquist, M. (1996). "Mariachi Conferences and Festivals in the United States." In E. Peterson, ed., *The Changing Faces of Tradition: A Report on the Folk and Traditional Arts in the United States*, 18–23. Washington, DC: National Endowment for the Arts.

Fogelquist, M. (2001). "Strings through Mariachi." *American String Teacher*, *51*(2), 57–61.

Fogelquist, M. (2002). "Mariachi Conferences and Festivals in the United States." In J. T. Titan & B. Carlin, eds., *American Musical Traditions: Latino and Asian-American Music*, 72–75. Vol. 5. New York: Schirmer.

Fogelquist, M. A. (2017). "Elevating My Chicana Feminist Consciousness through the United States' First Female Show Mariachi." Master of Music thesis. University of Texas, Rio Grande Valley.

Fogelquist, M. (2021). "The Ingredients for a Successful Mariachi Program in Your School." *International Journal of Mariachi Education and Performance*, *1*(May), 59–64. Mariachi Education Press.

Fregoso, L. (1979). "Mariachi Music: An Ethnomusicology." Guests: B. Faulkner, D. Sheehy, H. Molina, & M. Fogelquist. Originally Recorded September 1. Center for Mexican American Studies. University of Texas, Austin. www.laits .utexas.edu/onda_latina/program?sernum=MAE_81_45_mp3&theme=Music.

Fuentes, R. (2008). "Rubén Fuentes Speaking about Mariachi in the US." Interview with R. Niebla in Guadalajara. Posted to J. Nevin's YouTube channel, February 28. www.youtube.com/watch?v=lolYZp04Dls.

Galindo, M. (1933). *Nociones de Historia de la Música Mejicana*. Vol. 1. Colima: Tipografía de "El Dragon."

Garrido, J. S. (1974). *Historia de la Música Popular en México (1896–1973)*. Mexico: Editorial Extemporáneos.

Garibay, O. (2017). "Towards a Hybrid Approach to Mariachi Education: Bridging the Gap between Formal and Informal Transmission of Musical

Culture." Master of Music project report. California State University, Long Beach.

Gaytán, M. S., & S. de la Mora. (2016). "Queening/Queering *Mexicanidad*: Lucha Reyes and the *Canción Ranchera*." *Feminist Formations*, *28*(3), 196–221.

GB Magazine. (2022). "Mariachi Museum." https://web.archive.org/web/20221209191809/https://gbsan.com/mariachi-museum/.

Geijerstam, C. Af. (1976). *Popular Music in Mexico*. Albuquerque: University of New Mexico Press.

Golarte, L. C. (2016). *Mariachi Nuevo Tecalitlán: una historia digna de contar (a Story Worth Telling)*. Guadalajara: Publicaciones Ilustra, S.A. de C.V.

Gómez Arriola, I. (2020). *Mariachi: Del Rancho a La Metropóli Global: Patrimonio Inmaterial De La Humanidad UNESCO*. Guadalajara: Taller Gráfica de Comala.

González, A. (dir.) (2004). *¡Viva el Mariachi!* Vision Quest Entertainment.

González, R. C. (2015). "Cátedra José Hernández: Respuesta integral a la recomendación de la UNESCO para la defensa del mariachi torreonense." In L. Ku, ed., *El Mariachi: Regiones e Identidades*, 309–17. Zapopan: El Colegio de Jalisco.

Google Arts & Culture. (2023). "Mariachi, Patrimonio de la Humanidad." https://artsandculture.google.com/story/mariachi-patrimonio-de-la-humanidad/DwVxmtyVLG4Dbw.

Gosling, M. & C. Simon (dirs). (2013). *This Ain't No Mouse Music! The Story of Chris Strachwitz and Arhoolie Records*. Sage Blossom Productions. https://web.archive.org/web/20231023051553/https://nomousemusic.com/.

Gradante, W. (1982). "'El Hijo Del Pueblo': José Alfredo Jiménez and the Mexican 'Canción Ranchera.'" *Latin American Music Review*, *3*(1), 36–59.

Gradante, W. (ed.) (2008). *Foundations of Mariachi Education: Materials, Methods, and Resources*. Vol. 1. Lanham: Rowman and Littlefield.

Gradante, W. (2015). "Las aventuras de un mariachero gringo: enseñanza de la música de mariachi en Estados Unidos de América." In L. Ku, ed., *El Mariachi: Regiones e Identidades*, 251–72. Zapopan: El Colegio de Jalisco.

Greathouse, P. (2009). *Mariachi*. Layton: Gibbs Smith.

Guerra, C. M. (2021). "Mariachi Programs at the University Level: Investigating Eurocentric Stereotypes." Master of Music thesis, University of Texas, Rio Grande Valley.

Gurza, A., with J. Clark & C. Strachwitz. (2012). *The Arhoolie Foundation's Strachwitz Frontera Collection of Mexican and Mexican American Recordings*. Los Angeles: UCLA Chicano Studies Research Center.

Harpole, P., & M. Fogelquist. (1989). *Los Mariachis!: An Introduction to Mexican Mariachi Music*. Booklet and CD. Danbury: World Music Press.

Heist, E. H. (1976). "Appendix: Border Music of the 1970s in the Southwestern United States." In C. Af. Geijerstam, ed., *Popular Music in Mexico*, 138–47. Albuquerque: University of New Mexico Press.

Henriques, D. A. (2006). "Performing Nationalism: Mariachi, Media and the Transformation of a Tradition (1920–1942)." PhD dissertation. University of Texas, Austin.

Henriques, D. (2011). "Mariachi Reimaginings: Encounters with Technology, Aesthetics, and Identity." In A. L. Madrid, ed., *Transnational Encounters: Music and Performance at the U.S.-Mexico Border*, 85–110. New York: Oxford University Press.

Hernández, A. D. (2014). "The Son Jarocho and Fandango Amidst Struggle and Social Movements: Migratory Transformation and Reinterpretation of the Son Jarocho in La Nueva España, México, and the United States." PhD dissertation. University of California, Los Angeles.

Hernández, R. V., I. B. Arroyo, J. A. Jimenez, Jr., A. Angel, & J. Clark. (eds.) (2022). *El Mariachi de México: Un Patrimonio Cultural para el Mundo*. Fundación Universitaria de Derecho, Administración y Política, S.C.: FUNDAp.

Hillard, G. (2009). "Mariachi Gives Students Hope for the Future." *NPR, All Things Considered*. www.npr.org/2009/02/01/99798089/mariachi-gives-students-hope-for-future.

Hippler, A. E. (1969). "Popular Art Styles in Mariachi Festivals." *American Imago*, *26*(2), 167–81.

Houston, R. (2018). "Susan Cashion." *Society of Folk Dance Historians*. https://web.archive.org/web/20230401134121/. www.sfdh.us/encyclopedia/cashion_s.html.

Howard, K., M. Swanson, & P. S. Campbell. (2014). "The Diversification of Music Teacher Education: Six Vignettes from a Movement in Progress." *Journal of Music Teacher Education*, *24*(1), 26–37.

IMDb. (2016). *El Gran Concierto de Gala del Mariachi*. www.imdb.com/title/tt7220960/.

Jáuregui, J. (1990). *El Mariachi: Símbolo Musical de Mexico*. Mexico: BANPAIS, Instituto Nacional de Antropología e Historia.

Jáuregui, J. (2001). *Un Antropólogo Estudia el Mariachi*. México: Consejo Nacional para la Cultura y las Artes, Instituto Nacional de Antropología e Historia.

Jordan, M. (2004). "Mariachi's Company Town." *Los Angeles Times*, January 30. www.latimes.com/archives/la-xpm-2004-jan-30-et-jordan30-story.html.

Jorgensen, D. L. (1989). *Participant Observation: A Methodology for Human Studies*. London: Sage.

Juarez, E. De Jesus. (2021). “Las Mariachis Suenan: How Mariachi Womyn Are Challenging Gender Norms through Their Collective Experiences.” MA thesis. California State University, Los Angeles.

Kalinec-Craig, C. A. (2015). “Uncovering the Mathematical Challenges and Connections When Using Mariachi Music as a Representation for Teaching Equivalent Fractions.” *Journal of Mathematics Education*, *8*(2), 4–21.

KCET. (1992). “Mariachi: A Tale of Three Lives.” *KCET's Life and Times*. https://archive.org/details/clloy_000015.

Kilpartrick, D., & L. Garcia. (ca. 1988). *Mariachi: Traditional Music of Mexico*. Unpublished manuscript. www.cpp.edu/class/music/docs/course-outlines/MU3112009.pdf.

Kim, S. J. (2013). “From El Mariachi to Spy Kids?: A Cognitive Approach.” In F. L. Aldama, ed., *Latinos and Narrative Media: Participation and Portrayal*, 195–210. New York: Palgrave Macmillan.

Ku, L. (ed.) (2014). *El Mariachi: Aprendizajes y Relaciones.* XII Encuentro Nacional de Mariachi Tradicional. Zapopan: El Colegio de Jalisco.

Ku, L. (ed.) (2015). *El Mariachi: Regiones e Identidades*. Zapopan: El Colegio de Jalisco.

Ku, L. (ed.) (2016). *El Mariachi: Danzas y Contextos*. Zapopan: El Colegio de Jalisco.

Ku, L. (ed.) (2017). *El Mariachi: Bailes y Huellas*. Zapopan: El Colegio de Jalisco.

Kun, J. (ed.) (2017). *The Tide Was Always High: The Music of Latin America in Los Angeles*. Berkeley: University of California Press.

Kurland, C. L., & E. R. Lamadrid. (2013). *Hotel Mariachi: Urban Space and Cultural Heritage in Los Angeles*. Albuquerque: University of New Mexico Press.

Laney College. (2023). “Juanita Ulloa.” Faculty page. https://laney.edu/music/faculty/juanita-ulloa/.

Las Cruces International Mariachi Conference. (2023). About Us. www.lascrucesmariachi.org/about-3.

LA Plaza De Cultura y Artes. (2023). “Corazón De La Comunidad: A Story of Mariachi in Los Angeles.” Exhibition held from May 15, 2015 to January 11, 2016. https://lapca.org/exhibition/corazon-de-la-comunidad-a-story-of-mariachi-in-los-angeles/.

LaValle, J. (1988). *El Jarabe: El jarabe ranchero o jarabe de Jalisco*. México: INBA Dirección de Investigación.

Lechuga, C. C., & M. Schmidt. (2017). "Cultural Straddling: The Double Life of a Mariachi Music Education Major." In B. C. Talbot, ed., *Marginalized Voices in Music Education*, 80–98. New York: Routledge.

Library of Congress. (2023). "National Recording Registry Inducts Music from Madonna, Mariah Carey, Queen Latifah, Daddy Yankee," April 12. https://newsroom.loc.gov/news/national-recording-registry-inducts-music-from-madonna–mariah-carey–queen-latifah–daddy-yankee/s/5a91b115-3825-4a5f-a702-35940b4de958.

Lipsitz, G., & R. Rodríguez. (2012). "Turning Hegemony on its Head: The Insurgent Knowledge of Américo Paredes." *The Journal of American Folklore*, *125*(495), 111–25.

Liu, F. Y. (2017). "The Impact of Mariachi Education on Academic Achievement in Tucson High Magnet School and Pueblo Magnet High School." Master of Music thesis, Tucson, AZ: University of Arizona.

Lopez, R. (2022). "¡Viva Mariachi! Mariachi Forever Stamps." https://web.archive.org/web/20220201131527/https://rafaellopez.com/2022/01/18/viva-mariachi-mariachi-forever-stamps/.

Loza, S. J. (1982). "Dissertation Critique: 'The Son Jarocho: The History, Style, and Repertory of a Changing Mexican Musical Tradition,' by Daniel E. Sheehy." *Aztlán*, *13*(1), 327–34.

Loza, S. J. (1982). "Origins, Form, and Development of the Son Jarocho: Veracruz, Mexico." *Aztlán*, 13(1), 257–74.

Loza, S. J. (1985). "The Musical Life of the Mexican/Chicano People in Los Angeles, 1945–1985: A Study in Maintenance, Change, and Adaptation." PhD dissertation. University of California, Los Angeles.

Loza, S. (1993). *Barrio Rhythm: Mexican American Music in Los Angeles*. Urbana: University of Illinois Press.

Madrid, A. L. (2013). *Music in Mexico: Experiencing Music, Expressing Culture*. New York: Oxford University Press.

Malone, G. (2019). "Can Someone Please Explain What's Up with the Japanese Mariachis?" *BeLatina*. May 17. https://web.archive.org/web/20230925224559/https://belatina.com/please-explain-whats-up-with-the-japanese-mariachis/.

Manna, M. (2010). "A by-the-book look at mariachi." *The San Diego Union-Tribune*. January 21.

Mariachi Channel. (2014). "Host Mia Perez Interviews Mariachi Historian Jonathan Clark." Five-Part Interview, Posted to YouTube, January 14. www.youtube.com/watch?v=sey-DGb3_74.

Mariachi Education Press. (2023). Homepage. https://web.archive.org/web/20230320050844/https://mariachieducationpress.com/.

Mariachi Los Camperos de Nati Cano. (2013). *Recuerdos de mi Vida: Con La Filarmónica de Querétaro*. CD. Los Angeles: Mariachi Los Camperos .

Mariachi Miracle. (2022). "The Mariachi Miracle: A Film/Book Project by Daniel Buckley." https://web.archive.org/web/20220820062558/http://www.mariachimiracle.com/.

Mariachi Scholarship Foundation. (2020). "History of the Mariachi Scholarship Foundation." https://web.archive.org/web/20230405090442/https://mariachischolarshipfoundation.org/history/.

Mariachi Scholarship Foundation. (2024). "Museo de Mariachi." Floorplan. https://web.archive.org/web/20240111014912/https://mariachischolarshipfoundation.org/museo-de-mariachi/.

Marquez, L. (2013). "The Magic of Mariachi." *UCLA Magazine*, October 1. https://newsroom.ucla.edu/magazine/mariachi-music.

Marsh, E. (2015). "El Gran Concierto, Mariachi Vargas de Tecalitlán." Posted to YouTube, October 18. www.youtube.com/watch?v=Wke4bsTwOBw.

Marsh, E. (2018a). "Mariachi Divas & Magiconcert Virtual Orchestra 'LA BIKINA.'" Posted to YouTube, October 13. https://youtu.be/JwDp4E1_gYU.

Marsh, E. (2018b). "Trio Ellas & Magic Concert Virtual Orchestra 'El Mercader.'" Posted to YouTube, October 9. www.youtube.com/watch?v=F6Ci2dF64Nc.

Marsh, E. (2019). "Musical Instrument Awarding Ceremony, Tecalitlán, Jalisco." Award ceremony, Public School #32, Tecalitlán, Mexico (October 10). Posted to YouTube, October 20. https://youtu.be/bE_5pF95tps.

Marsh, E. (2021a). "KPBS Interview – Ed Marsh & José Ronstadt." Posted to YouTube, June 27. https://youtu.be/CEgECq5A9oM.

Marsh, E. (2021b). "El Gran Concierto – FULL." Posted to YouTube, June 27. https://youtu.be/gab4yv9TSqc.

Marsh, E. (2022). "Mariachi (Historia * Estrellas * Leyendas) Exhibit – Southwestern College Library." Posted to YouTube, December 13. www.youtube.com/watch?v=3bw9TCm8Ah0.

Marsh Library. (2013). *Mariachi Vargas de Tecalitlán: A Gift, an Honor, a Glory.* Also Featuring Mariachi Divas de Cindy Shea. Vargas' First Appearance in Rosarito, October. CD.

Marsh Library. (2014). *Grammy Jammin' x Mariachi Divas & Mariachi Espectacular de Beto Jimenez*. Two-DVD set.

Marsh Productions. (2015). *El Gran Concierto de Gala del Mariachi, with Bi-National Symphony Orchestra from Mexico and USA*. Program Guide, 75 pp, December 12.

Marsh Productions. (2016). *El Gran Concierto de Gala del Mariachi: Mariachi Vargas de Tecalitlán*. Recorded Live with the Bi-National Symphony Orchestra, Baja California Center, Rosarito Beach, B.C., Mexico, December 12, 2015. DVD and Blu-ray versions.

Marsh Productions. (2018). *The MagiConcert Virtual Orchestra*. Courtesy of Marsh Productions. https://drive.google.com/file/d/1cESwZn87ydUJOgXEurZCcqhYv5GWyGnx/view?usp=sharing.

Marsh Productions. (2022a). "El Gran Concierto de Gala del Mariachi." https://web.archive.org/web/20220106082330/http://thebigconcert.com/.

Marsh Productions. (2022b). Homepage for Marsh Productions. https://web.archive.org/web/20220409053351/http://marshproductionsinc.com/.

Mariachi Spectacular. (2022). "2022 — Mark Fogelquist." Mariachi Music Hall of Fame, Albuquerque, New Mexico, February 15. https://mariachispectacular.com/2022-mark-fogelquist/.

Mariachi Spectacular. (2023). "Mariachi Music Hall of Fame." https://mariachispectacular.com/hall-of-fame/.

Martínez de la Rosa, A. (2014). "Bailes de pano, diablos y negritos: Relaciones musicales y dancísticas entre México y Perú." In L. Ku, ed., *El Mariachi: Aprendizajes y Relaciones*, 213–30. Zapopan: El Colegio de Jalisco.

Martínez, F. (2023). "Latinx Files: When 'Mariachi' Went to Sundance." *Los Angeles Times*, January 26. www.latimes.com/world-nation/newsletter/2023-01-26/latinx-files-mariachi-documentary-latinx-files.

Martínez, M. (2012). *Mi Vida, Mis Viajes, Mis Vivencias: Siete Décadas De La Música Del Mariachi*. Conaculta: Dirección General de Culturas Populares.

Martínez, M., & J. Clark. (2012). "Miguel Martínez: Patriarca de la Trompeta Mariachera." In A. Camacho, ed., *Memorias del coloquio*, 317–40. Zapopan: El Colegio de Jalisco.

McMurtrey, M. (1987). *Mariachi Bishop: The Life Story of Patrick Flores*. San Antonio: Corona.

Medrano, A. (2019). Interview by Maggie Rivas-Rodríguez, December 17. Voces of Mariachi Collection, University of Texas, Austin. https://voces.lib.utexas.edu/collections/stories/anthony-medrano.

Mendoza, V. T. (1956). *Panorama de la Música Tradicional de México*. México: Universidad Autónoma de México.

Mendoza, A. (2022). "Herederos del mariachi participarán en concierto a beneficio de organización local." *The San Diego Union-Tribune*, July 1. www.sandiegouniontribune.com/en-espanol/espectaculos/eventos/articulo/2022-07-01/leyendas-del-mariachi-a-gala-concert-to-benefit-mariachi-scholarship-foundation.

Mijares, G. (2022). "TONIGHT: Mariachi Scholarship Foundation launches Ed Marsh Mariachi Museum Exhibit in Chula Vista." *Chula Vista Today*, July 15. https://web.archive.org/web/20231201023408/https://www.chulavistatoday.com/local-news/tonight-mariachi-scholarship-foundation-to-launch-ed-marsh-mariachi-museum-exhibit-in-chula-vista/.

Monaghan, P. (2007). "El Profesor de Mariachi." *The Chronicle of Higher Education*, May 25. *53*(38), 52.

Mount Royal University. (2023). "Mary-Lee Mulholland." www.mtroyal.ca/ProgramsCourses/FacultiesSchoolsCentres/Arts/Departments/SociologyAnthropology/Faculty/Mary-LeeMulholland.htm.

Morales, O. (2013). "Review: World's Best Collegiate Mariachi Remains a South Bay Jewel." *The Sun*. Southwestern College, May 14. www.theswc-sun.com/review-worlds-best-collegiate-mariachi-remains-a-south-bay-jewel/.

Moreno, R. M. (1961). *Apuntes sobre el pasado de mi tierra*. México: Costa-Ámic.

Morgan-Thornton, A. M. (2021). "Analysis of Texas Collegiate Mariachi Ensembles: Standard Repertoire and Genres." Doctor of Music Education thesis. Lynchburg, VA : Liberty University.

Mulholland, M. L. (2004). "Mariachi and Mexican National Identity." *Canadian Diversity*, *3*(2), 81–84 (Spring).

Mulholland, M. L. (2007a). "Mariachi in Excess: Performing Race, Gender, Sexuality, and Regionalism in Jalisco, Mexico." PhD dissertation. Toronto: York University.

Mulholland, M. L. (2007b). "*Mariachi*, Myths and *Mestizaje*: Popular Culture and Mexican National Identity." *National Identities*, *9*(3), 247–64.

Mulholland, M. L. (2013). "A Beautiful Thing: Mariachi and Femininity in Jalisco, Mexico." *Anthropologica*, *55*(2), 359–72.

Mulholland, M. L. (2021). "Jalisco Is Mexico: Race and Class in the Encuentro Internaciónal del Mariachi y la Charrería in Guadalajara, Mexico (1994–2003)." *Journal of American Folklore*, 134(533), 292–318.

Munguía, R. D. (2018). "The Impact of Mariachi Instructional Programs on the Son de Mariachi among Student Mariachi Ensembles." MA thesis. California State University, Northridge.

Nájera-Ramírez, O., N. E. Cantu, & B. M. Romero. (eds.) (2009). *Dancing across Borders: Danzas y Bailes Mexicanos*. Chicago: University of Illinois Press.

National Endowment for the Arts. (2023). "NEA National Heritage Fellows." www.arts.gov/honors/heritage/list?title=sheehy&field_year_value=All.

NATS. (2018). "Mariachi in Your Studio?" Breakout Session with M. Neel & M. Fogelquist. *National Association of Teachers of Singing*, June 23. https://web.archive.org/web/20230928072257/https://www.nats.org/_Mariachi_in_Your_Studio_.html.

NBC News. (2012). "'Mariachi Has Changed My Life': Mexican Music Grabs US Students," May 4. www.nbcnews.com/news/world/mariachi-has-changed-my-life-mexican-music-grabs-us-students-flna753615.

NPR. (2012). “This Mother’s Day, Strike Up the Band.” *Tell Me More*, May 10. www.npr.org/2012/05/10/152422157/this-mothers-day-strike-up-the-band.

Neira, J. C. (2014). “Reflexiones acerca del impacto sociocultural que genera la inserción de la música mexicana de mariachi en el nororiente colombiano.” In L. Ku, ed., *El Mariachi: Aprendizajes y Relaciones*, 259–70. Zapopan: El Colegio de Jalisco.

Neufeld, S., & M. Matthews. (eds.) (2015). *Mexico in Verse: A History of Music, Rhyme, and Power.* Tucson: University of Arizona Press.

Nevin, J. (2002). *Virtuoso Mariachi*. Lanham: University Press of America.

Nevin, J. (2006). *Mariachi Mastery: La Maestria del Mariachi*. Harp/Arpa. San Diego: Neil A. Kjos Music Company.

Nevin, J. (2016a). *Mariachi Mastery: La Maestria del Mariachi*. Trumpet. San Diego: Neil A. Kjos Music Company.

Nevin, J. (2016b). *Mariachi Mastery: La Maestria del Mariachi*. Score with CDs. San Diego: Neil A. Kjos Music Company.

Nevin, J. (2016c). *Mariachi Mastery: La Maestria del Mariachi*. Armonia. San Diego: Neil A. Kjos Music Company.

Nevin, J. (2017a). *Mariachi Mastery: Songbook*. Armonia (Guitar and Vihuela). San Diego: Neil A. Kjos Music Company.

Nevin, J. (2017b). *Mariachi Mastery: Songbook*. Guitarron (Cello & Bass/ Chelo & Contrabajo). San Diego: Neil A. Kjos Music Company.

Nevin, J. (2019). *Mariachi Mastery: La Maestria del Mariachi*. Armonia (Guitar and Vihuela). San Diego: Neil A. Kjos Music Company.

Nevin, J. (2022). “Orígenes musicales del son de América Latina y del Mariachi.” In R. V. Hernández, I. B. Arroyo, J. A. Jimenez, Jr., A. Á. “El Cuervo,” & J. Clark, eds., *El Mariachi de México: Un Patrimonio Cultural para el Mundo*, 111–28. Fundación Universitaria de Derecho, Administración y Política, S.C.: FUNDAp.

Nevin, J. & N. Sanchez. (2006). *Mariachi Mastery: La Maestria del Mariachi*. Score. San Diego: Neil A. Kjos Music Company.

Ochoa, Á. S. (2000). *Mitote, Fandango y Mariacheros*. 3rd ed. Zamora: El Colegio de Michoacán and El Colegio de Jalisco.

Ochoa, Á. S. (ed.) (2001). *De occidente es el mariache y de Mexico: revista de una tradición*. Zamora: El Colegio de Michoacán and Secretaría de Cultura de Jalisco.

Ochoa, Á. S. (2015). *La música va a otra parte: mariache México-USA*. Zamora: El Colegio de Michoacán

Olsen, D. A., & D. E. Sheehy. (eds.) (1998). *The Garland Encyclopedia of World Music*. Vol. 2: South America, Mexico, Central America, and the Caribbean. New York: Garland.

PBS. (2003). *Mariachi: The Spirit of Mexico*. Documentary directed by Leo Eaton.

Pearlman, S. R. (1984). "Standardization and Innovation in Mariachi Music Performance in Los Angeles." *Pacific Review of Ethnomusicology, 1*, 1–12. https://ethnomusicologyreview.ucla.edu/sites/default/files/prevol1_0.pdf.

Pearlman, S. R. (1988). "Mariachi Music in Los Angeles." PhD dissertation. University of California, Los Angeles.

Pedelty, M. (1999). "The Bolero: The Birth, Life, and Decline of Mexican Modernity." *Latin American Music Review, 20*(1), 30–58.

Pedroza, L. (2017). "Latin Music Studies at Texas State University: The Undergraduate Minor in Mariachi and Its Implications for Expansive Curricula in Mainstream Institutions of the United States." In R. D. Moore, ed., *College Music Curricula for a New Century*, 135–54. New York: Oxford University Press.

Pérez, L. X. (2002). "Transgressing the Taboo: A Chicana's Voice in the Mariachi World." In N. E. Cantú & O. Nájera-Ramírez, eds., *Chicana Traditions: Continuity and Change*, 143–66. Urbana: University of Illinois Press.

Peterson, K. (2017). "Viva Mariachi!" *Acoustic Guitar*, 44–47.

Plana, T. & B. Rosario. (1999). *Much Ado about Nothing: Mariachi Style*. Adapted from W. Shakespeare. East Los Angeles Classic Theatre, Los Angeles, California. August 10.

Quintanilla, M. (1995). "Mariachi Queen: Laura Sobrino and Her Band are Breaking Barriers." *Los Angeles Times*, September 17. www.latimes.com/archives/la-xpm-1995-09-17-ls-46869-story.html.

Quintero, M. A. S. (2015). "Estudio del mariachi como un atractivo turístico tras su patrimonialización." In L. Ku, ed., *El Mariachi: Regiones e Identidades*, 291–99. Zapopan: El Colegio de Jalisco.

Rafael, H. (1983). *Origen e Historia del Mariachi*. Mexico: Editorial Katun.

Ramirez, E. (2023). "Harvard Has a Mariachi?!" Student Voices, February 21. https://college.harvard.edu/student-life/student-stories/harvard-has-mariachi.

Ricketts, W. K. (2013). "Mariachi as a Music Education Genre: A Study of Program Status, Pedagogical Practices, and Activities." Doctor of Musical Arts dissertation. Boston: Boston University.

Rivera, R. (2021). "How to Keep Your Mariachi Students Motivated during Online Learning." *International Journal of Mariachi Education and Performance, 1*(May), 23–27. Mariachi Education Press.

Rodríguez, G. S. (2000). "The History of the Tucson International Mariachi Conference: Library of Congress Bicentennial, 1800–2000: Local Legacies

Report." Tucson: University of Arizona Mexican American Studies & Research Center. www.tucsonmariachi.org/wp-content/uploads/2018/04/history-timc.pdf.

Rodríguez, R. (2005). "Mariachi Music." In S. Oboler & D. J. González, eds., *The Oxford Encyclopedia of Latinos and Latinas in the United States*. New York: Oxford University Press, 66–61.

Rodríguez, R. C. (2006). "Cultural Production, Legitimation, and the Politics of Aesthetics: Mariachi Transmission, Practice, and Performance in the United States." PhD dissertation. University of California, Santa Cruz.

Rodríguez, R. C. (2009). "Folklórico in the United States: Cultural Preservation and Disillusion." In O. Nájera-Ramírez, N. E. Cantu, & B. M. Romero, eds., *Dancing across Borders: Danzas y Bailes Mexicanos*, 335–58. Chicago: University of Illinois Press.

Rodríguez, R. C. (2010). "Politics of Aesthetics: Mariachi Music in the United States." In N. E. Cantú & M. E. Fránquiz, eds., *Inside the Latin@ Experience: A Latin@ Studies Reader*, 193–209. New York: Palgrave Macmillan.

Rodríguez, R. C. (2015). "Mariachi." In E. Zolov, ed., *Iconic Mexico: An Encyclopedia from Acapulco to Zócalo*. Santa Barbara: ABC-CLIO Greenwood, Vol. 1, 346–55.

Rodríguez, R. C. (2023). "Mariachi Accompaniment: Cultural Bearers for Communal Conviviality." *Twentieth-Century Music*, 1–29. https://doi.org/10.1017/S1478572223000038.

Rodriguez, C. & C. Ayala. (2023). "*Pura Alegría*: Young Adult Musicians Learning Mariachi in Schools and Participating in the Las Vegas Mariachi Scene." In J. Johnson, ed., *The Possibility Machine: Music and Myth in Las Vegas*, 70–79. Urbana: University of Illinois Press.

Romero, B. M. (2001). "La Creciente Popularidad del Mariachi en Los Estados Unidos al Final del Siglo XX." In Á. Ochoa Serrano, ed., *De occidente es el mariache y de Mexico: revista de una tradición*, 171–79. Zamora: El Colegio de Michoacán and Secretaría de Cultura de Jalisco.

Ronstadt, L. (1987). *Canciones de Mi Padre*. CD. Elektra/Asylum Records.

Sacolick, R. (2016). "Transcendence and Son Jarocho as Practiced in the San Francisco Bay Area." PhD dissertation. University of California, Santa Cruz.

Salazar, L. C. (2011). "From Fiesta to Festival: Mariachi Music in California and the Southwestern United States." PhD dissertation. University of California, Los Angeles.

Salazar, L. C. (2015). "Mariachi Music as a Pathway to Higher Education in the United States." *The Journal of the Vernacular Music Center*, *1*(1), 1–4. https://jovmc-ojs-ttu.tdl.org/jovmc/article/view/4.

Salazar, L. C. (2023). Personal website. Homepage, with CV. www.laurynsalazar.com/.

Saldívar, G. (1934). *Historia de la Música en México*. México: Secretaría de Educación Pública, Publicaciones del Departamento de Bellas Artes.

Samaniega, F. (ed.) (2020). *Mariachi: Entre La Tradición y la Innovación*. El Colegio de Jalisco / Secretaría de Cultura del Gobierno de Jalisco.

San Diego International Mariachi Summit. (2022). *Mariachi: Historia, Estrellas, Leyendas*. Magazine Produced by the Mariachi Scholarship Foundation for the inauguration of the Ed Marsh Mariachi Exhibit, Southwestern College, July.

Sands, K. M. (1993). *Charrería Mexicana: An Equestrian Folk Tradition*. Tucson: University of Arizona Press.

Saunders, L. (1976). "The Son Huasteco: A Historical, Social, and Analytical Study of a Mexican Regional Folk Genre." PhD dissertation. University of California, Los Angeles.

Sautter, B. (1993). "Gringo Star." *The Washington Post*, October 3. www.washingtonpost.com/archive/lifestyle/magazine/1993/10/03/gringo-star/cc726e35-832a-4dff-9da5-5ead345b7d33/.

Sebastian, J. P. (2022). "Rosarito Philanthropist Recognized for His Support of the Mariachi Culture in Tecalitlán." *Baja Times*, October 16–31. https://web.archive.org/web/20240111162814/https://www.bajatimes.com.mx/online/2022/10_16-31/pdf/magazine.pdf.

Schippers, H. (2015). "Applied Ethnomusicology and Intangible Cultural Heritage: Understanding 'Ecosystems of Music' as a Tool for Sustainability." In S. Pettan & J. T. Titon, eds., *The Oxford Handbook of Applied Ethnomusicology*, 134–56. New York: Oxford University Press.

Schippers, H. & C. Grant. (eds.) (2016). *Sustainable Futures for Music Cultures: An Ecological Perspective*. New York: Oxford University Press.

Schmidt, M., & M. Smith. (2017). "Creating Culturally Responsive Ensemble Instruction: A Beginning Music Educator's Story." *Bulletin of the Council for Research in Music Education* (Fall 2016 / Winter 2017), 61–79. https://www.jstor.org/stable/10.5406/bulcouresmusedu.210-211.0061.

SDSU. (2013). "Library Receives $2.25 Million Sci Fi Collection." *San Diego State University News Center*, January 29. https://newscenter.sdsu.edu/sdsu_newscenter/news_story.aspx?sid=74043.

SDSU. (2015). "World-Renowned Mariachi Vargas Concert Benefits SDSU." *San Diego State University News Center*, December 8. https://newscenter.sdsu.edu/sdsu_newscenter/news_story.aspx?sid=75951.

Sheehy, D. (1979). "The 'Son Jarocho': The History, Style, and Repertory of a Changing Mexican Musical Tradition." PhD dissertation. University of California, Los Angeles.

Sheehy, D. (1997). "Mexican Mariachi Music: Made in the U.S.A." In K. Lornell & A. K. Rasmussen, eds., *Musics of Multicultural America: A Study of Twelve Musical Communities*, 131–54. New York: Schirmer Books.

Sheehy, D. E. (1998). "Mexico." In D. A. Olsen & D. E. Sheehy, eds., *The Garland Encyclopedia of World Music*. Vol. 2: South America, Mexico, Central America, and the Caribbean, 600–25. New York: Garland.

Sheehy, D. (1999). "Popular Mexican Musical Traditions: The Mariachi of West Mexico and the *Conjunto Jarocho* of Veracruz." In J. M. Schechter, ed., *Music in Latin American Culture: Regional Traditions*, 34–79. New York: Schirmer Books.

Sheehy, D. (2002). "Curator's Introduction." In *Viva el Mariachi! Nati Cano's Mariachi Los Camperos*. Washington, DC: Smithsonian Folkways Recordings.

Sheehy, D. (2006). *Mariachi Music in America: Experiencing Music, Expressing Culture*. New York: Oxford University Press.

Sheehy, D. (2016). "Mexican Mariachi Music: Made in the U.S.A." In K. Lornell & A. K. Rasmussen, eds., *The Music of Multicultural America: Performance, Identity, and Community in the United States*, 137–59. Jackson: University Press of Mississippi.

Sheehy, D. (2018). "How the First LGBTQ Mariachi Became an Outlet for Advocacy." *Smithsonian Magazine*, November 14. www.smithsonianmag.com/smithsonian-institution/how-first-LGBTQ-mariachi-became-outlet-advocacy-180970789/.

Sheehy, D. (2019). "The Making of a Maestro: Mariachi Los Camperos Leader Chuy Guzmán." *Smithsonian Center for Folklife & Cultural Heritage*, August 21. https://folklife.si.edu/magazine/mariachi-los-camperos-leader-chuy-guzman.

Sheehy, D. (2021). "The Quarter-Century Reign of Mariachi Reyna." *Smithsonian Magazine*, March 30. www.smithsonianmag.com/blogs/smithsonian-center-folklife-cultural-heritage/2021/03/30/reign-of-mariachi-reyna-de-los-angeles/.

Sheehy, D. (2023). "Chris Strachwitz: A Life." *Smithsonian Center for Folklife & Cultural Heritage*, May 23. https://folklife.si.edu/magazine/chris-strachwitz-tribute.

Sinta, V. (2020). "*De viva voz*: Mariachi Musicians Share Their Stories." *US Latina and Latino Oral History Journal*, *4*, 5–44.

Smith, V. L. (2018). "The Influences of a Mariachi Education on Student Perceptions of Academic Achievement, Academic Attainment, and Student Engagement." Master of Music thesis. Stockton, CA: University of the Pacific.

Smithsonian. (2023). National Museum of the American Latino. Homepage. https://latino.si.edu/.

Smithsonian Global. (n.d.). "Daniel Sheehy (Dan)." https://global.si.edu/people/daniel-sheehy-dan.

Smithsonian Folkways. (2010). *Lessons in Mariachi Performance: The Sounds of Mariachi, featuring Nati Cano's Mariachi Los Camperos*. DVD and booklet, with Liner Notes by M. Fogelquist and D. E. Sheehy. Washington, DC: Smithsonian Folkways Recordings.

Smithsonian Folkways. (2022). "El Fanático de la Música Norteña: Chris Strachwitz and Arhoolie Records." Posted to YouTube. www.youtube.com/watch?v=IKeZYSWJUzU.

Smithsonian Folkways. (2024). "Free Resources for the Classroom." https://folkways.si.edu/learn.

Society for Ethnomusicology. (2018). "Interview with Daniel Sheehy (Smithsonian Folkways Recordings)." Posted to YouTube, October 23. www.youtube.com/watch?v=RtdNXyaEewc.

Sosa, O. (2018). *Los Güeros de la Sierra*. Bloomington, IN: Xlibris.

Southwestern College. (2023a). "Music – Mariachi Specialization." https://web.archive.org/web/20240111164722/.https://catalog.swccd.edu/associate-degree-certificate-programs/music/music-mariachi-specialization-aa/.

Southwestern College. (2023b). "Hispanic Serving Institution (HSI)." https://web.archive.org/web/20230811040449/https://www.swccd.edu/administration/office-of-student-equity-programs-and-services/resources/hispanic-serving-institution-hsi.aspx.

Southwestern College. (2023c). "Southwestern College Breaks Ground on $101 Million Student Union." https://news.swccd.edu/2023/03/southwestern-college-breaks-ground-on-101-million-student-union/.

Sperry, G. (2006). *Mariachi for Gringos: Unlocking the Secrets of Mexico's Macho Music*. San Diego: Amigo del Mar Press.

Sperry, G. (2011). *Mariachi for Gringos II: Discovering More of Mexico's Hottest Songs and Stories*. San Diego: Amigo del Mar Press.

Spitzer, N. (2002). "Mexican Mariachi." In J. T. Titan & B. Carlin, eds., *American Musical Traditions: Latino and Asian-American Music*, 69–71. Vol. 5. New York: Schirmer.

Stevenson, R. (1952). *Music in Mexico: A Historical Survey*. New York: Thomas Y. Crowell.

Strachwitz Frontera Collection. (2023). Homepage. https://frontera.library.ucla.edu/.

Suarez, J. (2017). "Fina Estampa: A Musical Journey through Mexico." MA graduate project. California State University, Northridge.

Sullivan, P. (2008). "Mariachi Rising." *Strings*, *23*(2), 55–58.

The Sun. (2014). "Mago de Mariachi Popularizes Mexico's Music." Southwestern College, April 25. www.theswcsun.com/mago-de-mariachi-popularizes-mexicos-music/.

Texas Tech University. (2023). "Lauryn Salazar, Associate Professor of Musicology." www.depts.ttu.edu/music/aboutus/faculty/lauryn-salazar.php.

Toor, F. (1985). *A Treasury of Mexican Folkways*. New York: Bonanza Books.

Toxqui, Á. (2015). "'That Mariachi Band and That Tequila': Modernity, Identity, and Cultural Politics of Alcohol Songs of the Mexican Golden Age Cinema." In S. Neufeld & M. Matthews, *Mexico in Verse: A History of Music, Rhyme, and Power*, 257–95. Tucson: University of Arizona Press.

Trachtman, I. & K. Connell (dirs.) (2012). *Mariachi High*. Rainlake Productions and PBS.

Traub, A. (2023). "Chris Strachwitz, Who Dug Up the Roots of American Music, Dies at 91." *The New York Times*, May 10. www.nytimes.com/2023/05/10/arts/music/chris-strachwitz-dead.html.

Trevio, L. (2001). "Mariachi Festival Brings Its Rhythms to San José." *SF Gate*, July 13. www.sfgate.com/bayarea/article/Mariachi-festival-brings-its-rhythms-to-San-Jose-2900997.php.

Tucker, E. (2020). "Museum Studies." In P. Leavy, ed., *The Oxford Handbook of Qualitative Research*, 517–40. 2nd ed. New York: Oxford University Press.

Tucson International Mariachi Conference. (2024). Mariachi Hall of Fame. www.tucsonmariachi.org/hall-of-fame/.

UCLA Today. (2013). "In Memoriam: Leading Music Scholar Robert M. Stevenson." *UCLA Newsroom*, January 3. https://newsroom.ucla.edu/faculty-bulletin-board/in-memoriam–leading-music-scholar-robert-m–stevenson.

UC Santa Cruz. (2019). "Russell Rodríguez, Assistant Professor of Music." https://music.ucsc.edu/people/russell-rodriguez.

Ulloa, J. (2009). *Canta mi son! Learn Spanish through the World of Mariachi*. CD/MP3 album. Vocal Power Productions.

Ulloa, J. (2018a). *The Gomezanda Mexican Song Collection: Songs, Arias, and Racheras*. Vol. 1. Fayetteville: Classical Vocal Reprints.

Ulloa, J. (2018b). *The Gomezanda Mexican Song Collection: Songs, Arias, and Racheras*. Vol. 2. Fayetteville: Classical Vocal Reprints.

Ulloa, J. (2018c). *The Gomezanda Mexican Song Collection: Songs, Arias, and Racheras*. Vol. 3. Fayetteville: Classical Vocal Reprints.

Ulloa, J. (2019). "Mexico's Mariachi Vocal Tradition." In M. Hoch, ed., *So You Want to Sing World Music: A Guide for Performers*, 126–43. Lanham, MD: Rowman and Littlefield.

Ulloa, J. (2023). "Juanita, the 'High Priestess of Operachi.'" *Juanita Music*. www.juanitamusic.com/.

Ulloa, J. (2024). *The Mariachi Voice*. New York: Oxford University Press.

UNESCO. (2011). "Mariachi, String Music, Song and Trumpet." https://ich.unesco.org/en/RL/mariachi-string-music-song-and-trumpet-00575.

United States Postal Service. (2023). "Mariachi Stamps," July 15. https://web.archive.org/web/20231227052648/https://store.usps.com/store/product/buy-stamps/mariachi-stamps-S_482304.

Urrutia de Vazquez, C., & M. Saldana. (1984). *Origen y evolución del mariachi*. Guadalajara: Guias Voluntarias de la Sociedad de Amigos del Museom.

UTSA. (2024). "The History of Music in San Antonio." *UTSA Libraries and the UTSA Institute of Texan Cultures*. https://lib.utsa.edu/samusic/.

Varga, G. (2013). "Women in Mariachi Shatter Stereotypes." *The San Diego-Union Tribune*, October 5. www.sandiegouniontribune.com/entertainment/music/sdut-groundbreaking-women-in-mariachi-2013oct05-htmlstory.html.

Vasquez, A. & S. Osborn. (dirs.) (2023). *Going Varsity in Mariachi*. Osmosis Films.

Virtuoso Mariachi. (2020a). "Jeff Nevin, Orchestral Conducting." https://web.archive.org/web/20240111165203/https://virtuosomariachi.com/jeff-nevin-orchestral-conducting/.

Virtuoso Mariachi. (2020b). "Mariachi Champaña Nevin." https://web.archive.org/web/20221219100801/https://virtuosomariachi.com/mariachi-champana-nevin/.

Virtuoso Mariachi. (2020c). "Mariachi Garibaldi: From Southwestern College." https://web.archive.org/web/20240111165604/https://virtuosomariachi.com/mariachi-garibaldi/.

Wagner, L. (2004). "Fundraising, Culture, and the U.S. Perspective." *Philanthropic Fundraising*, *46*, 5–12.

Westbrook, D. A. (2022). *L. Ron Hubbard and Scientology Studies*. New York: Cambridge University Press.

YurView. (2022). "Mastering the Art of Mariachi Music at Southwestern College." Posted to YouTube, September 19. www.youtube.com/watch?v=CzI7yctO1d0.

Acknowledgments

I am indebted to everyone who spoke or corresponded with me in preparation for this work as it evolved over the last three years: the musicians, scholars, community organizers, and visionaries who are helping support, shape, and preserve mariachi today. Several scholars and researchers pointed me to valuable sources and helped shape this project. In this respect, thanks in particular are due to Jeff Nevin, Jonathan Clark, Daniel Sheehy, Mark Fogelquist, Russell Rodríguez, and Juanita Ulloa. I also wish to express my gratitude to the US-Mexico Border Philanthropy Partnership in San Diego for funding that made this research possible and to Edward E. Marsh for his continued support of this project and mariachi education, both in the United States and Mexico. Finally, I am deeply thankful to Mervyn Cooke, editor of the "Music Since 1945" series, for feedback and shepherding this Element through to publication.

I dedicate this work to the next generation of mariachi musicians and mariachi studies scholars. The future is interdisciplinary and bright – and it is yours.

Cambridge Elements

Music Since 1945

Mervyn Cooke
University of Nottingham

Mervyn Cooke brings to the role of series editor an unusually broad range of expertise, having published widely in the fields of twentieth-century opera, concert and theatre music, jazz, and film music. He has edited and co-edited *Cambridge Companions to Britten, Jazz, Twentieth-Century Opera*, and *Film Music*. His other books include *Britten: War Requiem, Britten and the Far East, A History of Film Music, The Hollywood Film Music Reader, Pat Metheny: The ECM Years*, and two illustrated histories of jazz. He is currently co-editing (with Christopher R. Wilson) *The Oxford Handbook of Shakespeare and Music*.

About the Series

Elements in Music Since 1945 is a highly stimulating collection of authoritative online essays that reflects the latest research into a wide range of musical topics of international significance since the Second World War. Individual Elements are organised into constantly evolving clusters devoted to such topics as art music, jazz, music and image, stage and screen genres, music and media, music and place, immersive music, music and movement, music and politics, music and conflict, and music and society. The latest research questions in theory, criticism, musicology, composition and performance are also given cutting-edge and thought-provoking coverage.
The digital-first format allows authors to respond rapidly to new research trends, with contributions being updated to reflect the latest thinking in their fields, and the essays are enhanced by the provision of an exciting range of online resources.

Cambridge Elements ☰

Music Since 1945

Elements in the Series

Music Transforming Conflict
Ariana Phillips-Hutton

Herbert Eimert and the Darmstadt School: The Consolidation of the Avant-Garde
Max Erwin

Baroque Music in Post-War Cinema: Performance Practice and Musical Style
Donald Greig

A Semiotic Approach to Open Notations: Ambiguity as Opportunity
Tristan McKay

Film Music in Concert: The Pioneering Role of the Boston Pops Orchestra
Emilio Audissino

Theory of Prominence: Temporal Structure of Music Based on Linguistic Stress
Bryan Hayslett

Heiner Goebbels and Curatorial Composing after Cage: From Staging Works to Musicalising Encounters
Ed McKeon

Understanding Stockhausen
Robin Maconie

The Queerness of Video Game Music
Tim Summers

Olivier Messiaen's Turangalîla-symphonie
Andrew Shenton

Chinese Émigré Composers and Divergent Modernisms
Chen Yi and Zhou Long

Mariachi in the Twenty-First Century
Donald A. Westbrook

A full series listing is available at: www.cambridge.org/em45

For EU product safety concerns, contact us at Calle de José Abascal, 56–1°, 28003 Madrid, Spain or eugpsr@cambridge.org.

www.ingramcontent.com/pod-product-compliance
Ingram Content Group UK Ltd.
Pitfield, Milton Keynes, MK11 3LW, UK
UKHW022143080726
473066UK00010B/729

* 9 7 8 1 0 0 9 4 6 1 3 6 8 *